# HAMILTON

M A S S A C H U S E T T S

# HAMILTON

## MASSACHUSETTS

### MYTHS, LEGENDS & A FEW QUIRKY CHARACTERS

ANNETTE V. JANES

Charleston    London

THE
History
PRESS

Published by The History Press
Charleston, SC 29403
www.historypress.net

Cover design by Marshall Hudson.

All photos are courtesy of the Hamilton Historical Society unless otherwise noted.

First published 2008

Manufactured in the United Kingdom

ISBN 978.1.59629.477.6

Library of Congress Cataloging-in-Publication Data

Janes, Annette V.
Hamilton : myths, legend and a few quirky characters / Annette V. Janes.
p. cm.
Includes bibliographical references.
ISBN 978-1-59629-477-6
1. Hamilton (Mass.)--History--Anecdotes. 2. Hamilton (Mass.)--History--Miscellanea. 3. Hamilton (Mass.)--Biography. I. Title.
F74.H17J36 2008
974.4'5--dc22

2008009762

All proceeds from this book will go to maintain the Hamilton Historical Society in carrying on its work and in hopes that we will someday be able to obtain a permanent home. For more information please visit us at Hamilton Town Hall, 577 Bay Road, Hamilton, Massachusetts, or write us at PO Box 108 Hamilton, Massachusetts, 01936. Our website is www.hamiltonhistoricalsociety.org and our email is hhs@hamiltonma.gov. Visiting hours are Thursdays from 1:00 p.m. to 3:00 p.m.

*This book is dedicated to my dear Johnny with love.*

*Hamilton:*

*The people are mostly engaged in agriculture for which the soil is well adapted; and lead very quiet, frugal, and contented lives. None of them are very wealthy; none of them very poor; and hence republican simplicity in the main prevails.*

—Standard History of Essex County, *1898*

# Contents

Preface                                                     11


PART I: MYTHS

The Masconomet Grave                                        14

The Lonely Grave                                            22

The Indian in the Swamp                                     24

The Stolen Boy                                              26


PART II: LEGENDS AND LORE

The Old Bay Road                                            28

Overseers of the Poor                                       34

Our Town                                                    37

The Myopia Hunt Club                                        40

Hamilton's Hotels                                           43

Drink or Dry                                                47

Asbury Grove                                                48

Fire! Fire!                                                 55

Asbury Grove Fire                                           59

Wigglesworth Cemetery                                       62

Quaint Poetry and Ancient Art                               63

Hamilton's Mills                                            67

Norwood's Mills                                             67

# Contents

Manning's Mills    70

Ice Industry    73

Starling Burgess's First Flight    79

Hey, We Move Anything!    80

Hamilton-Wenham Community House    82

Mingo Corner    84

School Days    85

Sulky Racing    89

Grass Rides    91

The Loud Cook    91

The Vanished Diner    92

PART III: QUIRKY CHARACTERS

Gail Hamilton    94

Colonel Robert Dodge    98

Samuel Wigglesworth    101

Manasseh Cutler    103

Joseph B. Felt    105

George L. von Meyer    106

Bradley Palmer    107

General George S. Patton Jr.    110

Helen Frick    112

Lady Nancy Astor/Nancy's Corner    113

Harrie Durham    115

Walter    118

Town Talk    120

Bibliography    125

# Preface

Researching this book has strengthened my belief of the good and dignified character of our town and its people. I have tried to give this historic material a bit of élan to pique the interest of readers. The chapters are only a thumbnail view. I hope that those who are interested in more information will check out our wonderful Hamilton Historical Society resources.

The chapters on Hamilton's Mills and the ice industry are based in part on lectures by Hamilton Historical Society's President ARTHUR "BUTCH" CROSBIE.

I am indebted to all past librarians and historians of the Hamilton Historical Society and others who took the time to file and record information on our town. Without this it would be impossible to reconstruct any part of town history. Special thanks to Edna Barney and Mary Anne Burridge, co-curators, and to Arthur "Butch" Crosbie, president of the society. Thanks, too, for oral material from Robert W. Poole, Robert A. McRae, Lawrence Lamson, Mary Anne Burridge, Edna Barney, Scott G. Janes, Veronica Sargent, Don Costin and others.

PART I

# Myths \ˈmiths\ *n.*

*Popular beliefs or traditions that have grown up*
*around something or someone.*

# The Masconomet Grave

When the ceremony ended that awesome day in November 1993, all who participated were deeply moved by what had happened. But the real story began over three hundred years before.

Hamilton, or the "Hamlet" as it was then called, was originally a part of the town of Ipswich and its history is intertwined. Hamilton did not separate from Ipswich until 1793, and Sagamore Hill, now in Hamilton, was once claimed by Ipswich.

On top of Sagamore Hill there is a grave that is of interest to both towns. There are two stones on the traditional site to commemorate the sagamore of the Agawam tribe. One reads:

> *Traditional grave site*
> *Indians of Agawam*
> *Masconomet Sagamore of the Agawams,*
> *Died March 6, 1658*

The other stone reads:

> *Musconominet*
> *Sagamore of the Agawam*
> *Died 1658*
> *Erected on the traditional*
> *Site of the grave by*
> *Heirs of W.H. Kinsman &*
> *J.F. Patch Le Baron 1910*

There are other spellings of this Native American name, too, but Masconomet is the most traditional. Whether the sagamore is buried in one of these exact spots no one knows for sure, but it is fairly well

The gravestone of Masconomet at the traditional site.

The gravestone of Masconomet erected by heirs of W.H. Kinsman.

documented that he is buried there on the hill. With a magnificent view of Ipswich Bay and Plum Island, it is a fitting and apt place of repose for one of the few known Native American graves in this region.

Located here too is the United States Air Force. It is both ironic and rather fitting that the U.S. Air Force Solar Observatory is also located on Sagamore Hill (only a short distance from the grave), as Native Americans revered the sun. The air force tracks solar flares because the radiation of the flares can interfere seriously with radio waves and communications around the world, with spaceships and with the welfare of astronauts in space.

Who was this Native American? There are many stories about him, some well documented in history and others surrounded by mystery and myth. This is an attempt to tell you his story as accurately as possible. There are some parts of the legend that are chilling and hard to believe and one part is rather eerie. But the tale is documented by historians and generally recognized as being as close to the truth as possible for the span of years it includes.

John Winthrop Jr. documented in his *History of New England, 1630 to 1649*, that when the ship *Arabella* sailed into the Ipswich Bay area in 1630, Masconomet and a friend paddled out to the vessel, boarded it and greeted its passengers in a friendly manner, settling in to visit for the day. The weary travelers were astonished to hear the sagamore speak a few words of English.

In historical documents, he is also referred to as Mashanomett, Musconominit and Masconnominet, and there are even other variations of his name. One historian's translation states that the meaning of the name is "man of great valor."

We tend to think of New England at this time as being remote and that the Native Americans were surprised to see ships, but in the very same book, Winthrop tells us, "We saw a ship lie there at anchor and five or six under sail up and down."

Many ships had been coming for years to the New World for the bountiful fishing. It is contact with very early visitors that probably caused the death of thousands of Native Americans from various diseases. Most historians point to smallpox as one of the illnesses that caused great devastation in a very short time.

Although it is estimated that at one time there were probably over thirty thousand native inhabitants in New England, around 1617, a mysterious plague had ravaged the people and only about one tenth of the population survived. By the time Winthrop and his followers arrived, vast fields that had been under cultivation were now empty of workers.

The natives in this area gave no resistance to the newcomers and there are many occasions when they were helpful. For instance, in 1619, when requested, Masconomet led David Thompson to Boston Harbor and helped him to choose a suitable island. He showed Thompson an island that was not occupied and that had the additional benefit of having all the fresh water that was needed for a family. Thompson's Island still retains the name to this day and is visited often by boaters and day-trippers.

There was a certain friendship between the settlers and the Native Americans that grew and there was mutual respect, for the most part.

About a year after the settlers arrived, Masconomet decided to raid a Tarratine village. The Tarratines, located on the other side of the Merrimack River, were the traditional enemies of the Agawam. They were fierce fighters and were reputed to be cruel to their enemies. It is unclear what had occurred between the two tribes before this attack, but Masconomet made a hostile foray into the Tarratine village, killing a number of their warriors and capturing some women and children.

The new settlers were very upset by what they felt was a malicious attack, and the general court ordered that Masconomet could not enter any Englishman's home for one year. A fine of ten beaver skins was levied for each time he broke this decree. This leads one to think that Masconomet and his followers must have spent a good deal of time in social contact with the settlers.

The Tarratines planned revenge and waited. Masconomet was at his lodge one evening with his friends Montowampate, Wenuchus and Wonohaquaham, being entertained with the astonishing adventures of Montowampate who had just returned from England, when the crafty Tarratines chose this time to attack the Agawam. Many of Masconomet's most valiant warriors were killed and several more were wounded. Montowampate's young bride was captured and brought to Maine.

Many of the natives in the village fled immediately to Governor Winthrop's home and begged him to save them because they said that the Tarratines were so brutal and pitiless that they always tortured their prisoners to death. According to the natives, one form of torture was to tie a prisoner to a tree and then have every member of the tribe bite a chunk of flesh from the piteous captive until nothing remained but the bones. Although it is reported that Governor Winthrop did not quite believe their story, he allowed them all to remain at his home.

Several more vicious forays by the Tarratines followed, centered on the towns of Ipswich and Lynn, and the colonists blamed Masconomet for everything that occurred. After all, they concluded, if he had not raided the Tarratines first, perhaps the Tarratines would not have become so hostile. It is doubtful that this was the case, but Masconomet's position was now much more vulnerable. When a directive came for all sachems (chiefs) to surrender their arms, it was a crippling blow to the natives.

Shortly thereafter, in June 1638, Masconomet sold all of his land to John Winthrop for twenty pounds, (the value roughly of about a hundred dollars). The territory at the time extended from the sea to Will's Hill in what is now Middleton, all of the land north of the Danvers River, Boxford, Ipswich, Topsfield and the whole of Cape Ann with the boundary of the Merrimack River.

In February 1644 Masconomet, along with Josias Chikataubet and Kutchamakin, signed a treaty putting himself, all his tribe and all his possessions under the protection of the Massachusetts Bay Colony and agreed to be instructed in the Christian religion. According to Joseph B. Felt's *History*

## DEED.

* "I Masconnomet, Sagamore of Agawam, do by these presents acknowledge to have received of Mr. John Winthrop the sum of £20, in full satisfaction of all the right, property, and claim I have, or ought to have, unto all the land, lying and being in the Bay of Agawam, alias Ipswich, being so called now by the English, as well as such land, as I formerly reserved unto my own use at Chebacco, as also all other land, belonging to me in these parts, Mr. Dummer's farm excepted only; and I hereby relinquish all the right and interest I have unto all the havens, rivers, creeks, islands, huntings, and fishings, with all the woods, swamps, timber, and whatever else is, or may be, in or upon the said ground to me belonging: and I do hereby acknowledge to have received full satisfaction from the said John Winthrop for all former agreements, touching the premises and parts of them; and I do hereby bind myself to make good the aforesaid bargain and sale unto the said John Winthrop, his heirs and assigns for ever, and to secure him against the title and claim of all other Indians and natives whatsoever. Witness my hand.

*28th of June,* 1638.

Witness hereunto,               MASCONNOMET,
    JOHN JOYLIFFE,
    JAMES DOWNING,
    THOMAS CAYTIMORE,          his    mark."
    ROBERT HARDING.

A land sale.

*of Ipswich, Essex and Hamilton*, his poignant and pitiable replies to questions reveal dramatically how powerless and weakened the natives had become.

> *Q. Will you worship the only true God who made heaven and earth, and not blaspheme?*
> *A. We do desire to reverence the God of the English and to speak well of him because we see He doth better to the English than other gods do to others.*
> *Q. Will you refrain from working on the Sabbath, especially within the bounds of Christian towns?*
> *A. It is easy to us—we have not much to do any day and we can well rest on that day.*
> *Q. Will you honor your parents and all your superiors?*
> *A. It is our custom to do so—for inferiors to honor superiors.*

With the tribe terribly weakened now, it is difficult to understand how any of the natives survived at all.

It was not until 1655, only three years before his death, that Masconomet was granted a small patch of four acres of land to cultivate. On March 6, 1658, he died and was buried along with his gun and other valuables as was the native custom. On June 18, 1658, according to Ipswich, Massachusetts town records, his widow was granted the land that he had fenced in.

Marked only by a stone, the site of his grave was known to locals and a curiosity arose about it. Only nine years later, according to the historian George Frances Dow in his *History of Topsfield*, two young men from Ipswich opened the grave of the sagamore and carried his skull on a pole (about the town ), "for which inhumanity one was made to sit in the stocks and pay a fine of 6.13.4 pounds." By the steep fine imposed, Felt suggests, we can deduce that the town fathers were horrified at this defilement, and the skull and other artifacts of Masconomet were quickly reburied.

But now, according to Native American belief, his spirit could not rest in peace. It is perhaps because of this desecration, and the shame to the local populace that it represents, that the gravesite has been traditionally noted and not completely forgotten as are most other Native American graves.

For years, blueberry bushes and wild brambles obscured the site, but then people began to recognize the significance of the grave and strove to treat it with the dignity they felt Masconomet deserved.

In 1969, Judge Standish Bradford, then Hamilton's town council, leased the Sagamore Hill area that he owned to the U.S. Air Force Observatory. They worked on an agreement that allowed the land on which the grave is situated to be a historical site.

At the time, Harold Daley was president of the Hamilton Historical Society. On May 2, 1969, in a document to the historical commission, Daley wrote:

> *In April of 1969, the Hamilton Selectmen established a Historical Commission. Judge Standish Bradford, owner of the property, donated the grave site to the Commission to insure the perpetuation of care for the grave of this one time leader of the original residents of this land.*

The plot of land is approximately 4,121 feet.

Through the judge's generosity, this agreement allows the spot to be a place of historical value that is opened to the public at times and on conditions determined by the commission, though it is not a public park.

After this, several articles in the local newspapers show some disagreement and complaint suggesting that the site was not well maintained. The Boy Scouts, the YMCA and the Hamilton Public Works Department at different times cleared and cleaned the area. Now the Hamilton Department of Public Works, along with the U.S. Air Force, keeps the site cleared of brush and debris.

Throughout the following years there were several public ceremonies observed at the site, some led by Robert Hagopian, and other more private rituals held by Native Americans.

In November 1993, there was an unusual ceremony that was moving, poignant and otherworldly. It started off simply enough. Mr. Robert Hagopian, and several people who had previously planned other ceremonies to honor Masconomet, organized a service to have the site of the grave consecrated because the Native American had become a Christian at the end of his life. It should be noted, however, that opinions differ among historians as to whether Native Americans became praying Christians by choice or coercion.

The public, along with special guests, was invited to the service together with historians, town representatives and Native Americans. A local clergyman was asked to do the Christian ceremony so that, in the Christian sense, the area would be a consecrated Christian graveyard and the town of Hamilton would then be responsible for its care. Chief Oeetash Roundtree of the Ponkapoag People, Massachusetts Nation, was invited to do the native ritual.

On November 6, 1993, it was one of those New England days when the sun was shining at its brightest in the morning after a downpour the evening before. There were few clouds in the sky and the promise of warmth in spite of the time of year. At Masconomet's gravesite, a large gathering of people stood around talking animatedly and greeting old friends as they waited for the ceremony to begin.

The ceremony began with speeches. Mr. Hagopian spoke first and then many others spoke, and these speeches continued for a good length of time. Then the clergyman began his ritual of blessing the site. This, too, took quite a long time. Throughout the ritual, those gathered together were respectful and quiet.

Then the ceremony by Chief Oeetash Roundtree began. In a letter addressed to the editor of the *Hamilton-Wenham Chronicle* the chief explained:

> *It is our belief when we change worlds that our spirit stays with our body. We as one then go to meet the great God of the Southwest, Katantowik in his gardens, from whence all good and beneficial things come. When our burial site has been desecrated, we believe that the Spirit of that person is called back to Mother Earth, where it will forever roam looking for its bones. Once found it still will not rest until proper burial ceremony is once more performed by our people. Today, November 6, 1993, three hundred and thirty five years after his death, Sachem Masconomet's Spirit is walking among us.*

The chief explained to all those present that he was not going to make a speech but instead would perform a sacred ceremony. He offered the sacred smudging stick to the Creator, the Four Directions and to Mother Earth. For Native Americans, the smudging stick is used to cleanse the spirit so that they may speak to the Creator with clean hearts, hands and minds. Then, Chief Oeetash Roundtree lit the sacred smudging stick and held it up to the Creator. At that moment crows began to call out from all directions, first one at a time and then all together in an awesome din. The sun was still shining in the sky, but it began to thunder.

The chief smudged his two companions, beginning at their heads and continuing all the way to their feet, and they did the same for him. Then he went in a circle all around the site. Next, he asked those present to hold hands and form a sacred circle around him and his companions. He told them that his friend Soaring Eagle would offer, to those who wished to participate, the sacred smudging stick ritual. While this proceeded, the cawing of the crows and the thunder continued in a strident din.

Next, they performed the sacred pipe ceremony and then walked again around the site scattering the ashes to Mother Earth, the Creator and the Four Directions. At the burial site they put sweet grass, sacred birch, tobacco and the remainder of the ashes from the pipe.

The ceremony of November 1993.

Suddenly, seeming to appear on a beam of sunshine, a chipmunk stood on its hind legs, chattering at the crowd. The thundering stopped and the crows ceased their calling. There was an awesome silence and then the chipmunk disappeared.

Chief Oeetash Roundtree wrote:

> *Now all within this sacred place is once again at peace. This then closes the final chapter on a once proud and noble Band of the Massachusetts Nation the Agawams.*

# The Lonely Grave

Much of the Hamilton landscape has changed from earlier times. What were forests and farmlands became house lots, parks and the downtown shopping area as change was accommodated. Some places that were well settled have reverted to forest and field. One only needs to walk any patch of woods around us to find stone walls that once were the boundaries of old homesteads.

There is a large field visible from Bay Road that is now part of the Appleton Farms Reservation. On old maps, the front part of this land is called the "Williams field" and the back part of it is called the "Tavern lot." Because of the stone walls and other signs of habitation, it is probable that there were other domiciles here too. Certainly there was the small house of Sarah Younger.

During the 1850s, when the railroad was being built, there was a tavern in this field that served the railroad workers and perhaps local farmers too. While construction on the railroad was going on, the tavern thrived, but it was never overly successful.

Close to this ancient cellar hole, overgrown with brambles and wildflowers and marked by a small headstone, there is the grave of Sarah Younger. Many hikers coming upon it pause to wonder why someone was buried in such an isolated place and to ponder the mystery of who she might have been. Why wasn't she buried in the cemetery?

Sarah was a woman who cooked for the railroad crews at the tavern, serving the many men, often transients, who frequented the place. One day in 1857 she became very ill and it did not take long to realize that she had smallpox.

At this time in New England there was no easy cure for most illnesses, and smallpox was a death sentence or a promise of terrible disfigurement to nearly

The lonely grave of Sarah.

all of those who were unlucky enough to catch it. There is an ancient curse that says "a pox on you," and that was about the worst thing you could wish on anyone. Smallpox was a serious matter. Once someone fell ill with smallpox, whole villages could become sick and many could die in a matter of days.

To prevent such an epidemic, and possibly to preserve the tavern business too, Sarah Younger's body was dragged out and quickly buried under cover of night. Then her home was set on fire and burned to the ground. There is no record stating that others contracted smallpox about that time, so perhaps the extreme precautions worked. Years later a Mr. William T. Lambert had a small stone erected on the site:

*Mrs. John (Sarah) Younger 1783–1855*

Yet one cannot help but think of what a sad and unique burial it was for a poor, hardworking woman.

It is interesting, though, to note that the tavern, or at least parts of it, is still in existence. Our forebears did not waste materials by throwing everything into dumpsters and starting anew. As Oliver Wolcott notes in *Down on the Farm*, records show that the tavern, though never a booming enterprise, continued for a while longer after Sarah's death. It was later moved to Bay Road, where it became part of the house at 1031 Bay Road, and perhaps part of the house at 965 Bay Road.

# The Indian in the Swamp

Once every two or three years, Hamilton Historical Society offers a bus ride around Hamilton with a narrator pointing out all the historical sites. A few years ago, while on this tour, Joanne Patton told this delightful story to those on the bus and she has graciously allowed us to repeat it here, reproduced from a letter written in December 2007. It is especially interesting because it shows how history is sometimes shaped with stories, while elements of the truth remain.

*Ruth Ellen Patton Totten* [Joanne's sister-in-law] *was a consummate storyteller. She was a prodigious student of history, of course, but she had great fun embellishing it, from time to time, especially for the pleasure of an audience. One of her favorite audiences was impressionable children and she always captured their attention with her presentations. In this case, she would be talking to children seated at her feet in our parlor, when they were on vacation or overnight guests. She would call their attention to a very large ash tree in front of this house with the circumference of several feet. About five feet up from the ground, there protruded from the trunk a heavy iron chain with about two feet of length hanging down that dated back to when settlers lived in our house and there were conflicts between the settlers and the local Indians. After one bad fight a settler from Green Meadow captured an Indian and chained him to the tree. Sometime afterwards however, the Indian got loose and the settler chased him across the road when the Indian fell into a pond and drowned. Ever since then, said Ruth Ellen, the spirit of the Indian came out of the pond looking for the settler. She said that the way anyone could know that the Indian had returned was when they found muddy handprints on the front door.*

*Now, invariably, the morning after the telling of that tale, Ruth Ellen would ask the visiting children if they would go out to the curb and fetch the morning paper. Soon, the adults at the morning breakfast table would hear screeches as the children ran back to tell them that the Indian had been there. They knew it because there were muddy handprints on the front door!*

An ash tree.

Mrs. Patton went on to say that about a year ago she was informed by Albie Dodge, our famous local arborist, that the tree had ash blight, and soon after, the tree died and had to be cut down. The rings in the tree proved it to be over a hundred years old. The Pattons have had the section of the tree with the chain hanging out of it preserved and will perhaps exhibit it at some time.

# The Stolen Boy

Nathaniel Woodbury, a resident of Hamilton was taken by Native Americans while visiting in Wells in 1712. After suffering many hardships, he and his family were able to pay a ransom of thirty pounds, a large sum for that time, and he returned home in November 1720.

He was given sixty pounds by the general court for his hardships and was later appointed as an interpreter of the sign language that was used at that time to facilitate communication between various tribes of natives and the Europeans.

# PART II

# Legends \ˈle-jənds\ *n.* and Lore \ˈlȯr\ *n.*

*Stories coming down from the past and traditional knowledge or beliefs.*

# The Old Bay Road

What historical riches we have around us! Route 1-A that runs through our town was at different times called the Post Road (for mail), the County Road (first state road), the Bay Road (coming from the Bay Colony, i.e. Boston) and Main Street (main road through town).

It began long ago as a Native American path when foot travel was all that was available. It was the first state road, laid out in 1640 in Hamilton through the farmland that was owned by Matthew and John Whipple. The road started in Hingham, ran around the "Great Pond" in Wenham and continued on to the coastal areas of Ipswich and Newburyport. The most challenging part of travel at the time was crossing the many brooks, streams, rivers and other bodies of water that are prevalent in New England. There was a bridge built across the Saugus River as early as 1639, but from Charlestown to Boston, a ferry had to be hired. By 1710, the Eastern Stage, a passenger coach, began running regularly from Boston to Newburyport along Bay Road, often stopping in our little town.

By 1726, the post or mail coach ran from Boston to Portsmouth through Hamilton. There are stone markers still preserved along the route showing the way and marking the distance to the next stop. Although it was once called Main Street in Hamilton, as it is still called in Wenham, in 1963 Hamilton voted to change the name back to Bay Road.

Along the side of this old Bay Road, a heinous murder occurred near Wenham Lake. In 1637, John Williams, a ship's carpenter, and John Hoddy had escaped from the Ipswich jail, where they had been imprisoned for theft. In a quarrel that arose between the two men not far from Wenham Lake, John Williams killed John Hoddy. There was swift justice at the time and Williams was hanged in Boston on September 28, 1637. It was the first murder among European people brought to court in Massachusetts.

Along this road, Joseph C. Felt reported in his *History of Ipswich, Hamilton and Essex*, wolves were so plentiful in the eighteenth century that parents were advised not to allow their children to walk to church alone lest they be snatched away. (Perhaps this infestation was similar to the plague of Canada geese we now have in Patton Park?)

On the old Bay Road in Hamilton, one spot that was an important hostelry and certainly a comfort to weary travelers from afar was the Old Brown Tavern (Whipple House) adjacent to the Hamilton Congregational Church. Though it is not certain, it is thought to have been built by John Whipple about 1690. At one time it was the home of Captain Daniel Brown, a blacksmith, tavern keeper and the town's first postmaster. Tradition has it that the sign outside the tavern read, "At the Sign of Governor Hancock." His son Israel was also a postmaster and tavern keeper and held many town offices.

If it were possible for us to see the ghostly presences of ancient travelers, it is very probable that we would see a middle-aged John Adams on an errand to the Ipswich Court, an important court at the time, perhaps accompanied by his friend Josiah Quincy. John Quincy Adams, John's son, also traveled up and down this road on his way to study law under Theophilus Parsons in Newburyport.

In 1775, a famous Hamlet Minuteman, Robert Dodge, along with a company of men, marched down Bay Road on his way to Medford to assist in routing out the British.

The Brown House.

From the nearby Congregational Church on Bay Road, our own Reverend Manasseh Cutler in 1787 blessed the departure of a large covered wagon and a group of forty-five people on their way to settle Marietta, Ohio. As an agent for the Ohio Company, a million acres of land had been purchased by Cutler for a dollar per acre. Later, in July 1788, Cutler himself ventured forth in a sulky to check the progress of the settlement and returned home within three months.

In all sorts of weather, as long as the road was passable, mail and passenger delivery coaches rushed through Hamilton. One summer day, President Monroe came to visit his friend Manasseh Cutler and stayed for a bit of supper.

It is reported that in 1825 General Lafayette, after traveling from Beverly in a frightful rainstorm over Bay Road, arrived at the Brown Tavern, shaking himself like a wet hen. And in a letter sent back to France and printed in the *Observer*, another Frenchman, Duke de la Rochefoucauld-Liancourt, declared that "this road is an uninterrupted garden, a delightful road."

The old Bay Road looking north toward Ipswich, 1895. *B.H. Conant Wenham Historical Association and Museum.*

All types of light and heavy, private and commercial carts and wagons filled with salt marsh hay, vegetables, salted alewives, corn, chickens, shoes, lace and many other products rumbled along on their way to and from Boston, Ipswich and Newburyport.

Imagine Bay Road as it was in the late 1800s with stately elm trees on either side arching over in a lovely shady canopy. Children on their way to the schools located on Bay Road and the pious on their way to church, all walked or rode this central thoroughfare that is still the main road through our town. There was a time when it was easy to spot several windmills along the way.

Until the coming of the railroad in 1839, the center of town was located in the vicinity of the Hamilton Town Hall and the Congregational Church, but the Wenham-Hamilton Depot, as it was then called, created an active business section in south Hamilton.

By 1886, horse-drawn streetcars made travel along this old road a bit easier when the Naumkeag Street Railway extended the line from Salem and Beverly to Asbury Grove. The town voted later not to allow the line to go as far as Moulton Street.

The Boston and Maine Railroad depot area showing the freight house, station, windmill, water pump, water tank and the Essex branch turnoff. *B.H Conant Wenham Historical Association and Museum.*

About 1895, most horses had been retired to the barns and meadows for a long rest. Electric cars (the Lynn and Boston Electric Railroad) moved into the same routes that the horsecars had pioneered. Shortly after that, a line ran to Ipswich via Essex Street and Sagamore Street (called Crooked Lane then), near the former Junction Ice Cream stand, and then branched out to Essex and Cape Ann. The lines ran alongside the roads, with turnouts built in where needed. These cars opened up a great change in the way people traveled. Few ordinary folks had cars then and records show that by changing frequently from different stops, one could go all the way to Portland and New York.

Along this road in more modern times we have seen joyful parades at the commemoration of Hamilton's centennial and bicentennial celebrations and many high school homecoming parades. We have witnessed countless Memorial Day parades as we honored veterans of the Civil War, World Wars I and II, the Korean War, the Vietnam War and other conflicts. Along this road, Hamiltonians have set off to joyful picnics at Crane Beach and traveled to the cemetery to pay their last respects to many friends and family members.

Old Bay Road after a storm, looking south, 1940. *Raymond A. Whipple photo.*

32

A comical incident involving the school committee took place on Bay Road in the year 1893. We would probably call it "hoodlumism" now. This particular series of events began when there was a serious lack of wood and kindling to heat the small schoolhouses around the town. It was reported in the newspapers that

> *the streets of the village were overrun by schoolchildren for the past two days, jumping onto sleighs and pungs and otherwise enjoying themselves as children do on a winter's day. This would not be noticeable on a Saturday, but when it begins on Thursday and continues into the week, curiosity is aroused.*

Apparently children were running wild and everyone in town had to keep dodging barrages of snowballs from these seventy-five unoccupied rascals.

The teachers, Miss J.F. Hastings and Miss Lucy Gray, were holding an "indignation meeting" and trying to locate other members of the school committee besides Mr. Lovering. Apparently Mr. Lovering, who was the school committee chairman, was in practical charge of procuring all needed school supplies. During Thanksgiving vacation he hauled a load of pine kindling to the schoolhouses, but did nothing about coal, and coal was what was needed.

The teachers kept school as long as the coal lasted, but when it ran out, they sent all the scholars home. Mr. Lovering, upon being interviewed, did not deny that the coal was low, but he said that there was plenty of fuel (kindling wood). He said he had ordered coal, but that the dealer could only supply him with one bushel, which could hardly start a fire in the large stoves that were used.

The taxpayers and parents were loud in their denunciation of him, claiming that the burning of kindling wood to heat two large school-rooms and the turning loose of seventy-five scholars and the services of two teachers for which the town had to pay was not right, nor was Mr. Lovering's complacency when he was informed of the state of affairs.

Mrs. Clifford (a school committee member) became sick with nervous prostration, and Mr. Knowlton, another school committee member, was in the center of town and could not be reached, so the matter was in the hands of the chairman. It was loudly claimed, according to the December 8, 1893 edition of the *Beverly Evening Times*, that by Mr. Lovering's inaction, he stirred up negative feelings that would show up at the annual town meeting in March.

# Overseers of the Poor

Life is full of unexpected events, both pleasant and less so, and nearly everyone can, through unfortunate circumstance, find that they are among the poor, unable to work or to care for themselves. In such a state, we are all at the mercy and compassion of others. Though present-day society sometimes complains that the less fortunate are not well treated, in comparison to the past, empathy today is far more in evidence. It is difficult to imagine living in the eighteenth and early nineteenth centuries and being in dire straits.

It was a New England custom in the earliest days to assist needy people only so far as to get them out of town as quickly as possible. If a poor unfortunate arrived in town, she would be given a little something and a ride over the border to the next town. Vagrants or newcomers were scrutinized and judged quickly.

According to Felt's *History*, in 1832–33, $516 were expended on fifteen paupers. He grumbled that most of the debt was brought on the community by intemperance, and that it (the money) was twice what the interest on a good farm would be.

A few years later, a comparatively more sympathetic board was formed called the Overseers of the Poor. Its function was to find out the family origin or earliest location of the vagabonds or poor and to send the unfortunates to those towns for help or to collect resources for upkeep. As can be seen in records, the overseer was not always unbiased in his judgment.

From a multicolored, mottled paper journal dated 1864 to 1898, now on file at the Hamilton Historical Society, the following entries for Hamilton residents are noted with names omitted. It is interesting to observe that though the overseers were very slow in correspondence (perhaps the postal service was at fault for this), they did not take a Christmas vacation. Though Christmas was observed at the time, it was nothing like the frenzied celebration that is now the custom. Written in thin, careful brown script are a few of the letters dating from 1864 to 1898:

> *Dec. 28, 1864*
> *To the Overseers of the Poor of the Town of Gloucester*
> *Gentlemen:*
> *M. whose legal settlement is in your town, but now residing in this town has made application to this board for her daughter L. alias H. and her four children who also reside in this town (they being in needy circumstance) for assistance which we have granted and charged the amount to the town of*

*Gloucester and shall continue to do so until you remove them or otherwise provide for their support.*
*For and in behalf of the Overseers of the Poor of the Town of Hamilton*
*Signed,*

*Note. M. is the widow of A. who belonged to Gloucester, said L. her daughter (after three or four illegitimate children) married one B. (who she says came from Gloucester) and who immediately left her.*

*Hamilton December 26, 1864*
*To the Overseers of the Poor in Marblehead*
*Gentlemen:*
*A., your pauper, now residing in this town, called on me today to write to you again for clouthing [sic] that he has received that you sent him for which they are all very thankful, but they are all of them destitute of under clouthing [sic], shirts and the like and are suffering. He needs a pair of boots very much as his old ones are past being worth mending he wares [sic] 9 size.*
*Yours truly,*
*One of the Overseers of the Poor of Hamilton*

*Hamilton December 16, 1866*
*To the Overseers of the Poor in the Town of Marblehead.*
*Gentlemen,*
*A. who resides in this town, but who belongs to Marblehead requests me to write you that he is in need of clouthing, [sic] for himself and his family and says that he must have them immediately or they shall freeze to death. He tells me they are suffering for all kinds of clouthing, [sic] and I should think that by the look of him and one of his children that I saw in the road the other day that he told the truth, for that one was certainly not fit to be seen out of doors.*
*Respectfully,*
*Signed,*
*One of the Overseers of the Poor.*

*Hamilton Sept 30, 1864*
*To the Overseers of the Poor in the Town of Gloucester*
*Gentlemen,*
*E. and family whose legal settlement is in your town, but now residing in Hamilton being in needy circumstances has applied to this board for*

*relief which we have granted and charged the same to your town and will continue to do so until you remove them or otherwise provide for their support.*
*Yours truly,*
*Signed,*
*One of the Overseers of the Poor*

*P.S. The aforesaid E. was the illegitimate son of one H. alias H. Said H. died in the Gloucester almshouse about 35 years ago and her son E. was bound out as a youth to T. by the town authorities of Gloucester. E. has lived in our town some years, but has never gained settlement by owning real estate or by taxation or in any other way.*

The following excerpts give a thumbnail portrait of Hamilton and illustrate how for some, hardship was a familiar companion:

*H. is a white woman apparently about 25 or 30 years of age; and is reported to be the wife of S. a colored man. She has been delivered of a child and he does not make his appearance to take care of her and pay expenses.*

*Will continue to board the K. children age six and four at $2.00 a week.*

*We utterly refuse to pay anything towards her support or to remove her or to pay charges that have accrued.*

*We find that her husband is working at the North Beverly Ice Houses and is doing well and will support her and the children if she will come back to the home. She took three dollars when she left,—but he has been steady and not drinking since,—so under the circumstances we positively decline to grant any assistance.*

*Find that they are unable to live for $3.00 per month.*

*Gentlemen, this is a matter of prompt action as the girl is expected to be confined at anytime.*

*D. is a colored man come from Nova Scotia about three years ago. He was choping [sic] wood in this town cut his foot very bad and is laid up with it. Think when he gets out he will take care of himself well enough.*

*Her husband a year ago got into difficulty and had to leave town. She has always worked as a servant in some family.*

# Our Town

In the beginning, for the people of Hamilton farming was the chief occupation. On average most farmers owned two to four horses or oxen, two to four cows, some heifers and some pigs. Some of the original farming family names were Adams, Brown, Dane, Dodge, Knowlton, Lamson, Lovering, Patch, Smith, Whipple and Woodbury. The size of these larger farms was from seventy-five to three hundred acres. Most owned smaller lots too for the cutting of firewood. Many of these families intermarried and some of their ancestors still remain in town or in the surrounding area.

The size of Hamilton is 9,593 plus acres. In 1865, 6,594 acres were under cultivation, providing evidence that just about all the arable land was in use with the rest being primarily rivers, ponds, wetlands and rocky outcrops.

The chief crops grown at first were corn and potatoes, but hay was by far the largest harvest. As the town population grew, the farmers began to raise commercial crops such as vegetables for market gardening and fruits such as apples, cherries, peaches, pears, plums and strawberries. Dairy farming and the keeping of poultry for sale purposes grew.

The people of this area were forward thinking. They often sought help to better their farms and orchards. As early as 1792, there was the Massachusetts Society for the Promotion of Agriculture. This was a group of men who believed that agriculture was the best way to make a living and that it could be improved with better plants and animals.

The farmers, always at the mercy of the New England weather, found that some years were certainly better than others. Sometimes everything went along smoothly and large crops were harvested, but not every year.

The year 1816 was a terrible time for farming in New England. Some called it the "year without a summer." Snow in a wind-driven blizzard fell on the newly planted fields on June 8 and halted the progress of all growing things. When the farmers had recovered from that and had planted another crop, snow fell again in July. Two more tempests made crops impossible for that year, so it was a lean time for those making a living from the land.

Livestock was important to the farmer. Different cattle breeds were introduced, as well as pigs, sheep and chickens. Better varieties of grain and corn were tried and adapted, and J.J.H. Gregory of Danvers introduced the cultivation of tomatoes by 1841.

By mid-1852, assistance was available to the farmers through the Massachusetts Board of Agriculture. In 1860, the Massachusetts Cattle Commission worked to help eliminate animal ailment. The Essex Agricultural Society held classes and lectures to help the farmers with growing hay, fruit cultivation, raising grain crops, raising livestock, improving the quality of poultry, raising specialties, ensilage, reclamation of land, forestry, arbor culture and combating insect enemies and the diseases of cattle, to name a few. Later, there were some choices for the ladies such as "the chemistry of the kitchen, our homes—their power and influence, the cultivation of heart's ease, and why a Massachusetts Farmer should be content."

Many new agricultural tools were introduced, a number of them because of Yankee ingenuity. Farmers now had a steel plow instead of iron and the revolving horse rake, and four-wheeled wagons took the place of the two-wheeled tip carts. There was "Raymond's Hay Elevator for moving hay into barns, the manure spreader, the disc harrow, True's potato planter, Willis' seed-sower, the Danvers truckle hoe and Chandler's horse hoe among others." Local farmers subscribed to new books on farming, farm periodicals, reviews from state agencies and analyses from the experimental station at Amherst

But soon, better-educated young people began to seek occupations other than that of a farm laborer. According to Janice Pulsifer in her book *Changing Town*, by 1911, the list of occupations in Hamilton consisted of carpenters, masons, blacksmiths, storekeepers, doctor, paperhangers, insurance agents, various businessmen, milk dealers, horse trainers, general building contractors and even a Chinese laundry located in a house on railroad avenue (Sing So Ho).

Now, women too had occupations outside of the home. At this time in a town directory, there were teachers, bookkeepers, store clerks, milliners and thirteen dressmakers in town. The number of dressmakers alone shows how ornate women's clothing must have been. When reading diaries or historic works of this time, over and over again there can be found a portrait of a people and village enjoying life to the fullest. In winter there were skating parties, sledding parties, ice races on the lakes, Christmas parties and gatherings of all kinds not just for children, but for those of all ages. In summer there were swimming parties, canoeing ventures, picnicking and teas.

There was a lot of change in a short time in the small town of Hamilton. The Myopia Hunt Club hunted for the first time in 1883 and purchased its

Hamilton in 1893. Linden, Willow and Home Streets are visible. Union Street has not yet been developed. Pictured is the Smith's block on Railroad Avenue, with a windmill behind it. *W.H. Conant Wenham Historical Association and Museum.*

property from the Gibneys (the former Dodge Farm) in 1891. The cost was $20,000 for over 149 acres of land with house and outbuildings.

The newcomers that were associated with polo saw the beauty and good location of Hamilton and began to purchase land and to buy up old farms. As new mansions and estates were constructed, the countryside changed considerably and the makeup of the town changed too. The various estates employed many townspeople, both skilled and unskilled. Some, like Bradley Palmer, sent to Italy for the professional stonemasons he employed for his estate and their skills are still in evidence all around us.

Irish maids moved to Hamilton from Ireland and Boston and later married and stayed on. French people from Canada and France came to work as cooks, dressmakers and milliners. Expert horsemen came to work from England and Ireland and they, in turn, settled here.

Many of these people brought with them a different faith, first meeting in what was then called Smith Hall on Railroad Avenue. Saint Paul's Catholic Church was built in part to accommodate these immigrants. The new people were a curiosity to the local Yankees and it took some time for both to adjust and for the newcomers to fit in. Both William Austin Brown and Gail Hamilton (Abigail Dodge), two prominent residents who kept diaries, comment on the newcomers, and not always favorably.

In comparison to the average frugal Hamilton inhabitant, the comings and goings of the new wealthy residents was a never-ending source of interest. In *Changing Town,* Pulsifer notes that native Austin Brown (1820–1908) kept a daily diary and log of all that was going on in his home and around the neighborhood, and from his work we can chronicle much of what was happening in town. He had kept an eye on the building of the Gardner Manor on Sagamore Farm Road in 1892. That year, he recorded that "Mr. Gardner comes today with his new bride."

The estates created new taxes for the town and did not really require any new services. In fact, many new, individual small businesses were generated to supply the common daily needs of these well-off folk. Except for a few disgruntled farmers, who muttered to themselves as the Myopia huntsmen galloped through their fields, there was reasonable accord.

One long-term benefit to the town has been that these estate properties held together a lot of acreage and this kept Hamilton looking rural and prevented the development of tract housing. Some of the estate owners have been generous in donating property for conservation and for the development of recreational and leisure activities such as walking trails, picnic grounds and wildlife observation.

# The Myopia Hunt Club

The townspeople of Hamilton can boast of a picturesque association within their community that is known as the Myopia Hunt Club. The very beginning of the Myopia Hunt Club's history is not in Hamilton, but in Winchester, Massachusetts (1879), when it was originally formed as a baseball, lawn and tennis club. Marshall K. Abbott, its first president, claimed that the club's chief fame at the time was for its delectable omelets and powerful "Myopia Punch." This brew's effect, he claimed, was responsible for the Myopia name. Other research points out that many of the founding members were myopic or nearsighted and that accounts for the interesting and now very famous name. Whatever the reason, the Myopia Hunt Club has contributed a lot of colorful history to Hamilton and has helped to keep Hamilton's landscape one of rural beauty. Considered the "sport of kings," there have been at least one prince and one princess and an American president who have visited Hamilton to participate in some way in the exciting horsemanship created at Myopia.

After a few years in Winchester, Frederick H. Prince, his three brothers and other friends and members decided to try fox hunting, and in 1881 the first hunt in this area was held at the Agawam House in Ipswich and at the Gibney Farm in Hamilton (1886). An English pack of hounds was brought from Warwickshire in England, and by 1885, ten pairs of beagles arrived to add to the fun. Now foxhounds are the dogs of choice.

The old Dodge/Gibney Farm was purchased in 1891 from John Gibney, a Salem sea merchant, and the club was then incorporated with the name of Myopia Hunt Club (1892). The first officers were Master Frank Seabury; Secretary Frederick Warren Jr.; and Treasurer George L. von Meyer. The stewards were Frederick Warren Jr., George L. von Meyer, Francis Peabody Jr. and Marshall K. Abbott. The first president, George L. von Meyer, was elected in 1893.

Wealthy people associated with the club began to seek summer residences and subsequently began to offer farmers hard cash for their lands. These Myopia folk from Boston's elite society recognized the fields and woods as ideal for the sport and purchased farms that were remodeled to suit them.

The first Myopia polo game was played on the Gibney Farm in 1888 in a rough pasture field, although there had been some attempt to roll it flat. A description of the first few games states that it was barbaric and reminiscent

The 1892 Myopia Polo grounds, now Pingree Park. *W.P. Kimball Wenham Historical Association and Museum.*

of a Native American skirmish. It points to the fact that skill had yet to be developed, and it is said that the local ambulance made frequent trips to the field. Surprisingly, though, they won the National Polo Association Championship in 1895. With few interruptions, polo is still played there now.

The colorful hunts are still held in Hamilton and the Thanksgiving Day chase is one of the most spectacular with the huntsmen's horns sounding the way. Fox are not sought after now. Instead, scent is laid along a trail for the foxhounds to follow. The scent is a concoction of red fox and coyote smells consisting of animal droppings, urine, mineral oil and water. It is wrapped in burlap, and about an hour before the hunt, it is dragged through the woods,

*Above:* The hounds at Myopia.

*Left:* A difficult jump.

fields, underbrush, meadows and swamps, usually by someone on foot. The hounds "give tongue" or cry madly as they begin to follow the trail of scent, and they can be heard for a mile away adding excitement to the fun.

The Myopia Hunt Club has sponsored or has been associated with over one hundred years of horse shows that have added color, prestige and enjoyment to Hamilton people.

# Hamilton's Hotels

For such a small town, Hamilton has had a variety of interesting hotels and accommodations. One selectman and overseer, Temple Cutler, advertised on April 25, 1816:

> *New Hotel in Hamilton*
> *The subscriber would inform his friends and the public that he has just opened the large and commodious three story house next door west of the meeting house in Hamilton, as a PUBLIC HOTEL, where he will be happy to accommodate all who may favour him with their custom. The house is pleasantly situated on the main road leading from Salem to Newburyport, and, with spacious and airy rooms offers a most agreeable and healthy residence to those gentlemen and ladies who may wish to spend summer months in the country. The Bar will be constantly supplied with the choicest of liquors, and the Larder with the best of provisions, varied by the season. Prompt and respectful attendance will be given at all hours, in the house and at the stable; and no efforts will be spared by the subscriber to give perfect satisfaction to all who may favor him in their patronage.*
> *Temple Cutler*

The location of this "new hotel" was the Wigglesworth/Cutler House. It would be interesting to see what would happen today if a hotel and bar opened up next door to the Congregational Church.

Other hotels built later seemed to favor Native American names. In Hamilton, there was the Chebacco House and the Winnepoyken; in Manchester, the Masconnomo House; in Ipswich, the Agawam House; and in Wenham, the Massasoit House.

There were at least four main hotels in Hamilton, some were year round and some seasonal, and each offered varying degrees of accommodations. There was the hotel at the Camp Meeting Ground in Asbury Grove and the Asbury House, a summer boarding hotel opposite Hamilton Park on upper Asbury Street. The Chebacco House and the Winnepoyken House were located on Chebacco Lake. The Hamilton House prospered at 1020 Main Street (Bay Road), and Clark's Boardinghouse/Hotel did business at a convenient railroad location on the corner of Walnut Street and Bay Road.

Some hotels were more elegant than others. Mrs. Clark for instance advertised that her thirty-five-cent dinners were her specialty and that she took in transients.

Hamilton House seems to have been quite popular and is said to have been gaily painted in several colors. Town officers celebrated here after an election with a "jubilee," and pleasant dancing parties were held here. The first-floor front rooms only accommodated spirits and intoxicating liquors.

The builder and first owner of the Chebacco House was John Whipple, the grandson of John Whipple who had once owned a vast tract of land in the area of Rock Maple Avenue and fought in the Revolutionary War. Young John had gone off to try his luck in the 1849 gold rush, but by 1859 he was back in Hamilton and had bought a farm on Chebacco Lake. The 1860 census lists show that he was living there and employed many servants. His sons carried on the business until 1889. The Chebacco House was located on a knoll of land between Beck's Pond and Chebacco Lake, now Villa Road, off of Chebacco Road. It was subsequently remodeled with tall pillars that supported the veranda surrounding it, thus allowing people to have a wonderful view of the lake. This accounts for its later name of Villa Veranda.

Local women were hired to cook and serve. Business must have been brisk because the menu was extensive, including lobster and "extra sirloin steak." It was a rather expensive place in a time when most working folks were making between $0.50 and $1.50 per day, and farmworkers less than that.

The restaurant was most famous for its chicken dinners and "unsurpassed cuisine." The half chicken fried à la Maryland, the half chicken sauté à la Creole and the half chicken sauté à la Marengo are all listed at $1.75. Potatoes and vegetables are separate servings at $0.50 to $0.75 each. One could be more frugal, though, and dine upon a cheese sandwich for $0.30 and a "jelly omelet" for $0.70. Coffee was $0.10 per demitasse, not exactly what a local farmer was used to. A picture of the desserts in the archives of the Hamilton Historical Society features cases full of delectable sweet choices.

There is a familiar Budweiser listed as a beverage at thirty cents, and also a scotch brew at thirty-five cents. The hotel boasted of a telephone connection, an important communication tool at the time, and advertised that the people coming into town from Boston could hire good conveyance at Cummings's livery near the train depot. In 1898, an advertisement appeared that boasted of "the chicken dinners for which the Chebacco House has for years been famous under the Whipple regime." Some records show that the chickens were cooked over wood fires, so that may have accounted for their popularity long before the age of barbeque. By 1892, the restaurant was owned by the Chebacco House Company and it continued the chicken dinner specialties.

New England weather is always changeable and often fickle, and so it proved to be on one hot August in 1878. Over 150 guests were enjoying themselves at the hotel, when an unexpected and very violent electric storm hit the building creating mayhem and sending the frightened guests into a state of chaos. Although there were no deaths, some were injured and the building needed extensive repair.

Chebacco House, later called the Villa Veranda, circa 1890.

By 1900, the property was owned by Frederick H. Prince, a multimillionaire financier and sportsman who began to acquire other properties in the area. After more than twenty purchases of land all around, including ponds and lakeside, he had amassed over a thousand acres. This vast acreage he called Princemere, and this is the property that was eventually purchased by Gordon College. The old hotel was torn down and that parcel of land was sold to a builder who constructed several homes in the ideal location.

The Winnepoyken House, was named for the son of Nanepashemet who was a famous sagamore of the Pawtuckets, once residing in the Salem area. This was located on the opposite shore of Chebacco Lake and was built in 1888 by Thomas W. Brown. It, too, advertised its famous chicken dinners. In 1908, John C. Rauch became the owner and changed the name to Lakecroft Inn.

Once again the advertisements boasted that the hotel was "personally managed by the man who made chicken dinners famous at the Old Cooper Tavern in Arlington." It went on to say that the rooms were large, the view unsurpassed, dinner could be had in the open air under the pines (no mention of mosquitoes), the roads were good for automobiles and there was boating, fishing and gunning in season. Stables and riding horses were available for hire. It was a large building, three stories high, opened year-round. In the stylish dining room guests could order lunch, tea and dinner, with steak and lobster another specialty and ten varieties of potatoes. By 1872 the Eastern

Winnepoyken House, later the Lakecroft Inn.

Railroad branch to Essex ran close by, helping to bring business to both of these hotels. The Winnepoyken Hotel is long gone, as is the railroad.

An interesting side note to the Chebacco House: it must have been considered the most elegant of dining places because it is here that, every year, Myopia Hunt Club hosted a dinner for the "farmers" of Hamilton. Special invitations were made and it became an annual affair around 1885. One can imagine being one of Hamilton's farm families waiting for this most prized of social events. (The farmers who allowed the Myopia huntsmen to ride through their fields were usually extended invitations to the events.)

At one time there was a conflict among the farmers and the Myopia Club members riding to hounds across their fields, but the master of the hounds Frank Seabury at the time was responsible for fostering good relationships. Invitation to compete in some field day sports at Myopia was extended to the farmers. The club also held picnics for the farmer's families at Centennial Grove in Essex and they also held harvest dances at the Chebacco House where it was said to be gaily decorated with Chinese lanterns. The Hamilton Town Hall was built in 1898 and shortly afterward, the Myopia Club hosted spring balls there for the young folks of Hamilton. It must have been lovely to see, as farmers, outstanding members of the community, Myopia members and attractive, prettily dressed young women walked with their escorts up the lovely curving stairs and into the dance hall there. (Some town offices are located in that area now.) According to Pulsifer in *Changing Town*, at these occasions estate owners, farmers and other local folk danced and enjoyed one another's company without class distinction.

# Drink or Dry

Though there were two notable hotels that served spirits, there were not many places where people could get liquor of any kind. Some years it was completely forbidden in Hamilton, when townsfolk voted to be "dry" and other times this would be overturned for a year or so. When the town was dry, it was strictly enforced.

Storekeeper and postmaster David M. Hoyt was the town's liquor agent, the sale of liquor being controlled by an agency under the state law (1862). He was licensed to purchase intoxicating liquors and to sell the same at his store "to be used in the Arts, or for Medicinal, Chemical, and Mechanical purposes and no other" (however that could be interpreted). Between 1875 and 1886, a first-class liquor license was issued to John and Samuel Whipple, owners of the Chebacco House, and to George H. Bishop and John R. Sargent for Hamilton House on Main Street and to Mr. Bishop for "drinking in the basement."

The townspeople by vote had the option as to whether to allow liquor. The ballot each year asked whether license should be granted for the sale of intoxicating liquor.

The vocal activity of the Women's Christian Temperance Union and the Anti-Saloon League pressured the Hamilton voters. From 1883 to 1910 the people voted "no" in fifteen out of the twenty-seven years. It was a serious topic at the time and divided the town. According to the *Wenham-Hamilton Times*, all the services at churches all over town were canceled on June 23, 1893, so that people would be free to attend the lecture of Mrs. Susan S. Fessenden, then president of the WCTU who spoke at the Hamilton Hall on Railroad Avenue and who "took strong prohibition ground overturning the arguments used by advocates of high license with an abundance of facts and superior logic."

The matter was still an important one in 1902, when according to the *Wenham-Hamilton Times* a raid was made by constables, deputy sheriffs and private detectives at the Winnepoyken House on Chebacco Lake, and at Frank Brown's at the four corners in East Hamilton. The search netted rye, whiskey, rum and other spirits that were "piled high in a wagon and hauled to town hall." There is no word as to what happened to it after that.

# Asbury Grove

A religious movement in the mid-1800s brought about another great change to Hamilton. Asbury Grove is named for the famous English pioneer circuit rider Francis Asbury (1754–1816) who answered the call of John Wesley for Methodist ministers in the United States at the young age of twenty-six. He is said to have traveled by horseback for forty-five years all over the country and he often preached three to five times per day. He was enormously successful in his dedication to the ministry and by the time of his death in

1816, he had ordained 3,000 Methodist ministers. By then it was estimated that there were about 250,000 Methodists in the United States.

Asbury Grove, located on Highland Street in Hamilton, is a unique and vibrant community that came about because of John Wesley and Frances Asbury's teachings. A group of Methodist ministers and laypersons from the Boston and Lynn areas found the pine groves and the rural setting beautiful and it inspired them to begin their special ministry there. Established in 1859, it is now called the Asbury Grove Camp Meeting Association, and though it began as a religious summer colony for tents and cottages, now there are many year-round homes there.

Beginning in the 1840s there were religious revivals that swept across the country, with especially strong movements and convictions in New England. In an interview in the *Beverly Times* on August 13, 1945, by Tim Johnson, the Reverend Willis P. Miller, longtime chaplain at Asbury Grove, stated:

> *Doctrines preached at camp meetings varied, but they had in common an emphasis on a sudden conversion experience among a group of people—Wesley's "social gospel." Camp meetings arose as a critique of the church. People felt the church was not emphasizing holiness enough, was not evangelizing fervently enough. There was a strong emphasis on personal salvation, personal commitment to Christ, combined with a stress on social justice and reform.*

Alcohol use was especially prohibited.

The entrance gate to Asbury Grove, circa 1907. *A.B. Norton Hamilton Historical Society.*

Asbury Grove still holds the record for being the oldest camp meeting ground of consecutive yearly meetings. The first preacher was the Reverend A.D. Merrill. The *Beverly Citizen* reported in June 1859:

> *The Committee who have had the business in charge, have bought ten acres of land including a pine grove about a mile from the depot for 600 dollars and have leased ten acres more. The Eastern Railroad Corporation have agreed to carry their baggage, committee, and ministers free and all others at half price.*

The land was purchased outright from the Dodges ten years later for $4,000. The Dodge house still stands at the entrance to Asbury Grove.

Though it started with only a few families housed in tents in 1859, it did not take long before the more convenient wood-sided tents were built over wooden frames. Straw was provided by the Asbury Grove managers to fill mattress ticks. By 1864, forty small, prefabricated houses were introduced and mixed in among the tents, and by the year 1899, the summer colony was close to three hundred unique little summer homes. Many were decorated artfully with pretty gingerbread trim.

Visitors to Asbury Grove in the early days.

50

Other large buildings were erected to accommodate the crowds. The Asbury Grove Association soon became a thriving and bustling community in the summertime, with its own stores, library, church, boardinghouses, laundry houses and restaurants. The Asbury Grove Camp Meeting became so renowned that a spur of the railroad was built to accommodate the worshipers. The popularity of the revival meetings was such that thousands attended, with the weekends especially jammed. Campmeeting Road off of Route 1 in Topsfield was the turn for travelers' wagons on the last leg of the trek to Asbury Grove in Hamilton. Crowds came on foot, by horse cart, bicycle, train, electric car, farm wagon and any other conveyance that could possibly be hired.

The *Beverly Citizen* reported on August 25, 1866:

> *The Camp Meeting during the week has been largely attended and the weather with the exception of Thursday has been all that could be desired. Many of those who were present on that day experienced a severe drenching during showers of the afternoon and evening. The Eastern Railroad has done a large and ruminative business in the transportation of passengers to and from Hamilton.*

Reportedly, crowds swelled to over fifteen thousand at one meeting. The original seating capacity inside Asbury Grove was for fifteen to sixteen thousand, and according to records, sometimes there was no place to sit. An article in the *Beverly Citizen* on August 10, 1867, states:

> *The Methodist Camp Meeting at Hamilton commences on Monday and continues through the week. The Eastern Railroad Company has made ample arrangements for the transportation of passengers, and will run* <u>*twelve*</u> *trains each way* <u>*daily.*</u>

It seems unimaginable for the town of Hamilton to have been able to cope with such a crowd. The population of Hamilton at the time was about eight hundred residents, so excitement must have been very high with so many newcomers.

The rules for the Asbury Grove community were fairly restrictive. Hours for preaching were 10:00 a.m., 3:00 p.m. and 7:00 p.m. The hour for rising was 5:30 a.m. and for retiring, 10:00 p.m. Hours for meals were 6:30 a.m., 12:00 noon and 5:00 p.m. Curfew bell sounded at 10:00 p.m. and after that there was to be no one out and no noise at all. A very useful rule was that at least one pail of water had to be at hand in case of fire. There was of course no running water at first. No card playing or dancing was allowed.

The chapel at Asbury Grove.

Though some people were able to bring their own food, cooking facilities were not always available and there were large dining halls to accommodate the crowds. To show how much was consumed at these plentiful dinners, there is an article from the September 2, 1877 *Salem Evening News* that states that a single Sunday meal could consist of 100 pounds of beef, 20 hams, 40 tongues, 15 lamb legs, 8,000 quarts of baked beans, 400 loaves of brown bread, 14 bushels of shell beans, 4,200 ears of corn, 7,200 biscuits, 600 quarts of pudding, 200 quarts of tea and coffee and 800 quarts of milk.

The first chaplain was the Reverend L.B. Bates, and the library within Asbury Grove was built in 1910, to commemorate his years of dedicated service. An avid reader, he had begun a collection of books for Grove residents. He inspired the Ladies Aid Society to raise $950, which was the cost of the structure, and to collect over a hundred books to stock it.

Theodore Johnson, a popular and well-respected man, was the superintendent of Asbury Grove for forty-seven years. According to reports from him, the Grove had its own police protection with a force of up to seven officers at times. In the beginning, there were some who came to the meetings to make fun and mock the worshipers, but this soon stopped, and though there were very large crowds, there was seldom any trouble.

*Right:* A small, steep-roofed Victorian cottage named "Woodland Rest" at Asbury Grove. *A.B. Norton Hamilton Historical Society.*

*Below:* Pleasant Avenue, with a hotel, restaurant and store, in Asbury Grove. *A.B. Norton Hamilton Historical Society.*

Swings and ball fields were later added for the children. There were tennis, street hockey and basketball courts, and horseshoes and volleyball fields. There was a wide walking path to Idlewood Lake, now called Pleasant Pond, where swimming, picnicking and boating took place. By 1959, a twenty-five-meter Olympic-size pool, eighty-five by forty-two feet with a wading area, was built for recreation within the Grove.

There was an active community of chapel groups, Bible schools, youth camps, ladies' aid and men's classes. The Couples Club later changed its name to Pairs and Spares, and later the Booster Club.

Facing the Lee Park area is the beautiful E. Stanley Jones Chapel, built in 1884 at the cost of $1,736. It was named for the outstanding Reverend Jones, an author and missionary to India who had preached in Asbury Grove. It has a steeple with a clock face and the letters Stanley Jones in place of the usual numerals to tell the time. Close by the chapel is the tabernacle that was used in rainy weather, and later for watching movies and for small theatre productions. There is an outdoor meeting area called the Vesper Circle with a gazebo-like structure that houses a pulpit open on three sides to face rows of benches. There was a large brick building that housed an active bakery. This area was later remodeled into a recreation hall and is

A view of the circle near the gazebo. *A.B Norton Hamilton Historical Society.*

now sometimes used for a thrift shop. It is interesting to note that it was the prudent Methodists who founded the Goodwill Industries.

The little paths among the cottages, originally only wide enough to allow the passage of a horse and buggy, are not much wider now and they contribute to the intimacy of the neighborhood. The cottages at Asbury Grove are treasures of Victorian architecture with little gables, gingerbread trim and welcoming country porches just waiting for an afternoon of lemonade and enjoyable conversation. Picturesque in so many ways, the Asbury Grove community has contributed a lot to Hamilton.

# Fire! Fire!

There have been some tragic fires in Hamilton—large barns, houses or estates have burned to the ground—but there are two major fires that are of particular note because of the multiple buildings destroyed, the vast areas devoured by flame and the valiant rescue work that followed. In the midst of chaos there were many incidences of heroism.

One major fire began on March 25, 1910, which happened to fall on Good Friday of that year. The fire began on Mill Street in a small, frame home occupied by the family of Charles E. Dodge.

Mrs. Dodge was attending to a sick child upstairs in the home when she thought she smelled smoke. When she went to investigate, she found that smoke was pouring from the cupboards around the apparently defective chimney. She rushed back upstairs to get her baby and other children. It was about noontime and a blustery March gale blew fiercely in a westerly direction. The fire quickly spread through the frame house and the howling wind spread ash, sparks and fire over other nearby homes. They soon became engulfed and the fire spread to more homes and then to businesses. Then, as if by magic, the fire seemed to spring up in other spots spreading all over through Mill, Willow and Asbury Streets and along the railroad track. It roared through the more settled town section and up Bay Road, eventually covering more than half a mile.

The fire department responded heroically and many people did what they could to deter the spread of fire, using buckets and brooms and pieces of evergreen to beat out the flames. But the wind-driven fire proved voracious as it raced down street after street, consuming all in its path.

The devastation of the March 1910 fire around Mill, Willow and Asbury Streets.

A large building that was soon engulfed was the Shamrock Hall, a great two-story structure that housed a dance hall upstairs and businesses below. A dozen wooden houses, other buildings, a laundry, sheds and garages were nearly instantaneously in flames.

Nearby, there were dog kennels owned by George S. Thomas with fifty expensive dogs howling as the flames crept closer. One dog, Encliffe Mite in a nearby kennel, was thought to be the most valuable dog in the entire canine world. But he was rescued, as were all the other dogs.

Opposite the corner of Mill and Willow Street, the property of Timothy Moynihan was entirely destroyed. Barns, coal sheds, houses, grain and hay storages and small outbuildings were consumed, including the large shipment of hay and grain Moynihan had just received. Across the railroad tracks, the entire Thayer estate, including houses, barns and outbuildings, was reduced to cinders in a matter of minutes.

The house and double barn on Main Street (Bay Road) in the area that is now called Patton Park, owned by Dr. Orran C. Cilley, was consumed by the fiery rage in a matter of minutes, and all that was left were the massive chimneys. Interestingly, when the fire on the roof began, the Cilleys were outside of their own home looking with interest at what was happening to others, not realizing that their own place had just caught fire too. Even the magnificent pine and fir trees that fronted the house were nearly instantly overwhelmed with raging flames.

There were no fire hydrants at the time and firefighters were drawing water from a nearby waterhole (in the area of Patton Pond) and from a natural depression that filled with water each spring at the end of what is now Cummings Avenue. Wells and cisterns were used too, but they were pumped dry in a matter of minutes. The blustery weather sent cinders far and wide, and soon all the dried fields around were in flames. Everything everywhere in the path of the fire was reduced to embers. Ash and soot filled the air, choking onlookers, firemen and others who were fighting the fires, as well as any nearby creatures.

Nearly three quarters of a mile away from the original holocaust on Mill Street, across the street and up from the Cilleys' residence, was the home of Jonathan Brown Jr. Sooty, hot ash ignited Brown's barn roof and men immediately climbed up to try to save it. The fire was small to begin with, but the raging wind and the immediate deposit of more flying red embers and fire made it impossible for them to do much. Soon, other buildings nearby were engulfed. Luckily, Brown's house was saved.

Although the fires did not consume any more buildings beyond this, the raging wildfires that had begun on the dry grasses and brush in the woods at the sides of the road raged on. It went as far as the Myopia Hunt Club and threatened the kennels, clubhouse and barns. Some spectators claimed that the advance of the wall of flame was similar to prairie grass fires that raged in the Great Plains from time to time.

The remains of Dr. Cilly's home on Bay Road, now the Patton Park area.

Downtown Hamilton in flames.

It was both an electrifying and unifying time for everyone in the area. Reports were that everyone from six to seventy-five years old was out fighting the fires with whatever was at hand, be it brooms, tree boughs or water buckets. Many offered their wells to firefighters, but they were used and drained dry in a few minutes and did not offer much relief.

Firefighters from other areas came to the aid of the weary Hamilton firemen. Wenham responded with the Enon #1. Ipswich sent its machinery over the road pulled by four sturdy horses. Beverly sent equipment and a chemical truck. Other apparatus arrived on the train from Salem, but these were not unloaded, as there was such scarcity of water and the fires were beginning to burn themselves out by then.

Home insurance was not as common then, but history notes that one large estate did have a policy with an agency in Hamilton by the name of F.W. Broadhead. Unlike modern insurance transactions, Mr. Broadhead viewed the damage and adjusted all costs before the smoke was completely cleared.

The firefighters had worked heroically throughout this conflagration, but they did not have a lot to work with. At the time of this fire, Hamilton still had only chemical extinguishers (hand-held fire extinguishers) and a horse-drawn hook and ladder. The ladders were stored at the west district schoolhouse, the horses were hired from a nearby livery stable and the fire call to alert the men was the ringing of church bells, so it is not difficult to understand why a major fire was a crushing disaster.

The total destruction of this devastating 1910 fire was twenty-five buildings and several businesses. Except for a few small pigs, there was no reported loss of life. However, a hundred people were left homeless and over fifty acres of land were left in smoky cinders.

There is one rather humorous story to come out of this tragic and chaotic fire. Apparently the fire hoses had been run across the railroad tracks in the excitement and turmoil of firefighting, and when an unexpected special rescue equipment train from Salem steamed into Hamilton, the hoses were cut in two, rendering them useless.

It is interesting that on this very same day there were other disastrous fires in several places. One nearby was in the small village of Essex, which was threatened by destruction when the same wind-driven March gale burned eight icehouses and then raged out of control, igniting adjacent trees and then burning massive old trees at Centennial Grove and the surrounding woods and fields.

# Asbury Grove Fire

Another major fire that swept Hamilton and caused a great loss of property was the fire at Asbury Grove in May 1927. Though there is some disagreement over what exactly caused the blaze, most reports claim that it was an oil heater that had been accidently overturned in an Asbury Avenue cottage.

Asbury Grove at the time was a close-knit Methodist Camp Meeting community just off of Asbury Street. It still remains much the same today, though there have been many changes and some of the homes are now year-round cottages.

Apparently, very dry conditions existed at the time of the fire, though there was no reported high wind. The cottages were so close together that once one began to burn, the flames easily spread to another. The fire occurred at a time when many people were preparing to open up their small summer homes. In all, over 119 cottages burned completely and another few were damaged. The scene of devastation was overwhelming. Furniture, bedding, tables, pianos and all kinds of things that make up a home were removed and placed outside the cottages as quickly as possible, but in the end, many of these things were destroyed too.

There were many acts of heroism as older folks were carried from the cottages and children were accounted for and moved to safer places. Others assisted in trying to save precious items such as furniture, daily necessities, photos and memorabilia.

Fire Chief Chester H. Knowles and A.A. Cummings were on their way home from Newburyport when they caught sight of the black cloud of smoke on the horizon. Reportedly, the chief said that he immediately knew that this was no ordinary fire. As soon as he arrived, he took command of the action and quickly called for out-of-town help. Many other fire departments responded to the call for assistance, with Wenham, Danvers and Beverly responding immediately and others responding a bit later.

Again, it was the lack of water to fight the raging flames that caused most of the problem. At one time the fire department tried using the many small wells and cisterns located there for the cottages to put out the flames, but this proved futile. Later, the Wenham Fire Department was able to hook up some lines to a nearby brook. There were over two miles of hose laid by various departments all over Asbury Grove.

Just half an hour after the fire began, the main gates to the grove were torn down so that fire apparatus and motor trucks being used to haul things away could move unhindered through the previously too-narrow gates.

A destructive fire at Asbury Grove, May 1927.

Hamilton Police Chief Arthur Southwick called out all his men, as well as a detail from the state constabulary force and a detail from the Beverly Police Department. The next day, the *Beverly Evening Times* reported:

*The buildings owned by the Asbury Grove Camp Meeting Association miraculously escaped destruction. The fire seemed to leap all around these buildings which housed the annual camp meeting. The natural auditorium under the tall trees which for years has been the scene of revivals, love feasts, and mammoth gatherings was miraculously saved, as well as the church houses including the Jesse Lee Hall of the First Methodist Church and the house formerly owned by the Swampscott Methodist Church, now a private home. The stand and the choir platform were left intact. The spacious tabernacle, the chapel which houses several thousand each season at camp meeting, hotel and Ladies Tea Room, the cook house and the John L. Bates Library all escaped the pathway of flames. The post office and the residence of the Superintendent of the Grove John R. Mann were also saved, as well as a row of cottages along the avenue leading down to the Association's barns and garage.*

*The back part of the Grove in the vicinity of Mt. Zion is all that remains of the cottages of the summer colony at Asbury Grove. Historical Mudge Avenue is still there, also Lee Avenue, Merrill, and Kingsley, but Asbury, Haven, Hamlin, Olin, Essex, Fletcher, Mt. Bellingham path, Prospect, Skinner and Hedding Avenues have just slipped out of sight, nothing but blackened dust and here and there a piece of charred furniture remains of what was once the prettiest section of Asbury Grove.*

*One of the distinct losses to the summer folks, especially the Ladies Aid Society, was the community house just on the outskirts of the circle. This was used by the society as a meeting place during the summer and was recently equipped with a piano and furniture which were destroyed—as was the Swedish tabernacle.*

After the fire, the police had trouble controlling the hundreds of curious sightseers and they had to screen the people they let in to be sure they were residents.

Within Asbury Grove there was no loss of life because the season was early and few had opened up their summer homes. But in the stress and excitement of the fire, there was one woman, only fifty-eight years of age, who was seized by a heart attack as she watched the fire from the hill on Asbury Street.

# Wigglesworth Cemetery

Just off of Bay Road there was an ancient burial ground called the Wigglesworth Cemetery, named after the Reverend Samuel Wigglesworth, an ordained minister and pastor of the Third Church of Ipswich in "the Hamlet," now known as Hamilton. Several prominent townspeople purchased a piece of land owned by the First Congregational Church for use as a private cemetery. Dedicated in 1850 with a program of singing, preaching and poetry, it was deemed a lovely spot, peaceful and sacred to all. But when the new cemetery across from the church on Bay Road was dedicated, the Wigglesworth Cemetery fell into disuse, and by 1910 it was an unattractive, uncared-for area of about 58,790 square feet of land.

In 1911, the park commission, led by Frank C. Norton and assisted by George L. von Meyer, was authorized by an act of the Massachusetts

The Cutler Park site of the former Wigglesworth Cemetery.

legislature to use the land as a park. All the bones, bodies, any remains in the graves, monuments and headstones were removed a bit farther up the road to what is now the Hamilton Town Cemetery on the other side of Bay Road.

As this was going on, many people and all the schoolchildren who were nearby were duly horrified by the disinterment, and many a tale arose from overactive imaginations.

The area was then turned into a park. Approximately one and a quarter acres were accepted in 1913 and the area was first called Central Park. Later, it was renamed by town vote "Cutler Park." It is seldom used by the public now, but it is still there, with beautiful views of Cutler Pond—a bucolic reminder of how things change all the time.

# Quaint Poetry and Ancient Art

Quaint, often poignant poetry and unique artistic carvings are present on many of the old headstones in Hamilton Town Cemetery. The oldest stone, though barely legible now, reads in part:

> *Memento mori, Fugit hora,*
> *Here Lyes ye Body of John Dane who departed this Life Dec., 23,*
> *1707.*

Some of the headstones feature verse that was quite obviously composed by grieving relatives. A number of the verses tell little stories, several are cautions to the passerby and others have a moral. The following are a few of the more interesting verses. In 1796:

> *Adieu my friends, dry up your tears,*
> *I must lie here 'til Christ appears*
> *My state is fixed, my glass is run*
> *My days are past, my life is done.*

This was written in 1856 for someone who was struck by lightning:

> *How sudden thine end*
> *Here with us today*
> *Ere tomorrow the angels*
> *Had borne thee away*

For an eleven-year-old are the words:

> *A breath, a gasp a groan or two*
> *And we are seen no more*
> *Yet on this brittle thread*
> *Hangs vast eternity.*

An ornate stone in Hamilton Cemetery, circa 1790s.

Written for a young woman in 1821:

> *Stop my young friends as you pass by*
> *And on my grave pray cast an eye*
> *Your sun like mine may set at noon*
> *Your soul be called for very soon!*

There are many other inscriptions that are equally poignant.

The Hamilton Town Cemetery has a lovely country setting with many venerable old trees, stone walls and shrubs. It is kept in beautiful condition by the Hamilton Department of Public Works. Every year there are at least two ceremonies held there honoring the men and women who have given their lives for our country and freedom. It is heartbreaking to see the rows and rows of military graves.

Skulls, vases and drooping trees adorn many old gravestones.

Both its isolation and quiet sometimes make the Hamilton Town Cemetery a refuge for vagrants and mischief-makers. Because of this, it is always patrolled by the Hamilton Police Department. Following is a modern-day spooky story told to me by one of Hamilton's finest.

*One night I drove into the cemetery for a look about as I was on my evening patrol. It is a small place, tranquil and well cared for with pine trees whose boughs hang long and low and old oak trees shadowing the paths. On the sides are woods and ferns and at the back there are a few graves that are situated outside of the main cemetery and further still a marshy area that borders the Miles River.*

*It was a beautiful spring evening, and the robins were repeating over and over the special four-note call they have sometimes. The sun had not quite set, yet a pale moon hung low in the sky. My cruiser window was open and I drove slowly around enjoying the spring air.*

*It was the time of evening when there is a pause between day and night; shadows are long and not clearly formed. In the peaceful silence I heard a thud and I thought it was perhaps someone digging. I stopped the car and listened and heard nothing, but after a few moments there was again a raspy, scratchy earth- and stone-moving rattle such as a spade might make on soft earth. A chill went up my spine and I felt my scalp itch. What was making such an uncanny noise?*

*I parked the cruiser and slowly got out. My flashlight revealed nothing unusual. I got back in the cruiser and waited a moment, and sure enough there was the eerie sound again. I got out again and moved quietly among the graves and suddenly, in the shadowy light on a distant grave, I thought I saw two little arms waving in the air. Two little arms! My eyes could not believe it. All kinds of visions came to mind, old horror movies and ghost stories, and risings from the dead.*

*I hurried back to the cruiser to get my light again and when I turned it on I saw to my amazement the shining eyes and beaky head of an enormous snapping turtle. She was imperturbably digging at the soft earth around an old grave. Now partially buried, little arms digging and waving, she had maneuvered herself into the earth to lay her eggs.*

*After all, it was spring and egg-laying time for snapping turtles, and in her reptile wisdom she had chosen one of the safest, quietest and least-disturbed places in all of Hamilton for her babies to be.*

# Hamilton's Mills

In the late eighteenth and early nineteenth centuries, the predominant occupation of Hamilton residents was farming, but there were two important mills in Hamilton that together employed about 160 people. There was also one very small family-owned mill. At a time when travel was difficult and farms were far apart, mills were an important meeting place for men, especially to exchange news and to visit a while.

The two large mills were the Manning or Willowdale Mills located on the Ipswich River in the Willowdale section between Hamilton and Ipswich, where the Ipswich River is the boundary. The road is called Winthrop Street on the Hamilton side and Willowdale Road on the Ipswich side. Then there were the large Norwood Mills located at the corner of Highland Street and Waldingford Road. On the corner of Bridge Street and Woodbury Street, there was a small sawmill owned by James Patch.

We have to try to envision what a deep, swift, formidable river the Ipswich River was at the time. No towns siphoned off the flow then as is the case now.

# Norwood's Mills

The Norwood mills were located on both sides of the Ipswich River, on Mill Street in Ipswich and Highland Street in Hamilton. As early as 1697, there was a log bridge here, built by the farmers who had adjacent property. Michael Joseph Farley was the owner of the first dam and gristmill. The mills were run by a waterwheel in the basement. Later, John Adams and his sons built a fulling mill on the north side of the river. In 1739, Caleb Warner purchased the property and built a mansion on the north side of the river. By 1767, Warner had added a sawmill to the gristmill.

In 1880, Caleb Norwood purchased the property from the Warners. Until 1912, the mill on the Ipswich side of the river produced isinglass, which is a substance made from the bladders of various fish. These were easily available from the fisheries of Ipswich and Newburyport. At the time, this type of gelatin was used in the clarification process of beer and wine and was made into some glues. Another type of isinglass was made from mica and was used as windows for parlor stoves, as it did not burn, and also for early automobile windows. The operation was conducted only in the winter months as it required icy cold water. It was rolled and pressed very thinly, hung up to dry and then put into barrels and carted to the Ipswich train depot for export. Local farmers provided all of the corn and wheat that was ground into flour at the gristmill, and a lot of cobs and corn were ground for animal feed.

Logs were carted to the river and stored in the water for a while to kill the insects. Then they were processed in a part of the mill where wood for packing crates, stove lengths and specialty hardwoods was made. Another product manufactured here was the wooden marsh shoes required as

The Highland Street home of C.J. Norwood, 1872.

equipment for horses harvesting salt marsh hay. The mill was well managed, as even the residual sawdust was used as an important component in storing ice. In local icehouses, the sawdust was placed between the huge ice blocks that were cut from neighboring ponds and lakes for the local ice trade.

The gristmill was converted to a cider mill that operated chiefly in the fall of the year. Approximately a hundred bushels of windfall apples would produce 350 gallons of cider, with the renowned Russet apple producing the tastiest. In the height of operation, more than ten thousand bushels of apples were consumed.

Several types of vinegars were produced too. This change, never as lucrative, was made during Prohibition, when there was a hue and cry against "hard cider." It was, in truth, just as intoxicating as any liquor if consumed in large amounts.

Most of the debris from this manufacturing process—apple pulp, fish residue, wood particles—was sluiced down the river and out to sea via the Ipswich River. The fish bladder dregs must have been a bit overpowering. Though apples have a sweet scent, the thousands of gallons of pulp must have been pungent and messy for those who lived along the river. By 1919, all operations had ceased on Hamilton's side of the Ipswich River. The mill building on Hamilton's side is still standing.

Norwood's Mill on Ipswich River, circa 1890.

Area of Norwood's Mill on Highland Street.

# Manning's Mills

In 1791 (two years before Hamilton separated from Ipswich), Dr. John Manning obtained a grant from the Town of Ipswich for a piece of land to build a woolen mill. Working with the Massachusetts legislature he was able to procure some financial assistance, and in 1794, he had constructed a large building 105 feet long, 32 feet wide and two stories high. Only the top part of the building was used for manufacture. The ground floor was used as a meeting hall and a law office for his son. A large windmill was constructed on a small tower above the building. This was the first time in America that wind power was used for manufacture. Called the Massachusetts Woolen Manufactory, the mill produced flannels and blankets and later, cotton. It was not a successful venture.

According to records, Dr. Thomas Manning received permission in 1824 to erect and maintain a dam three miles above the stone bridge at the fording place between Hamilton and Ipswich for grist or other mills, factories, et cetera. By 1829, Dr. Manning had built a dam on the river and constructed a wooden sawmill that burned soon afterward. He built another sawmill and used it, in part, for sawing veneers. By 1834, he had built a more substantial stone building and installed the factory now called Manning's Mills. He also constructed a boardinghouse for workers and some other small buildings.

Dr. Manning died in 1854. His heirs carried on, but by 1861 the mills were named the Agawam Woolen Company. Records from 1864 show that during the Civil War a lucrative mill was manufacturing woolen socks and goods. Later, the operation was called the Willowdale Manufacturing Company and its chief product was woolen blankets. By now, a whole village of small homes had been constructed in the area to house the workers. Unfortunately, in January 1884 a huge fire destroyed the mill and it was never rebuilt. The foundation of the mill can still be seen along the sluiceway from the dam to the mill. Manning's Mills was the largest industry Hamilton has ever known.

In 1895, six mill houses from the area, four small and two larger ones, were purchased by George M. Adams, grandfather of Edna Barney, co-curator of Hamilton Historical Society. The houses were lifted onto a truck with a series of wooden wheels placed under each corner and connected by ropes. It took six horses to pull them to the new location on the Mill Street property owned by Mr. Adams. At the time, it was easier to move a house than to build one and was much less costly. According to an old Hamiltonian, these houses were for rent for many years at ten dollars per month.

The stone boardinghouse was torn down and the stones were used for other house foundations and septic systems. One house next to the town hall has a foundation built of stones from Manning's Mills.

Although there is another river that cuts its leisurely way through Hamilton on its way to the Ipswich River, the Miles River was always too slow-moving even in the earliest days to accommodate mills with efficiency.

A view of Willowdale Mills, with school, stores and village.

Ruins of the woolen mills at Willowdale.

The remains of waterworks at the site of Manning's Mills at Willowdale.

A boardinghouse for millworkers at Manning's Mills.

Early records show that owners whose farms bordered its banks worked together each year to clear debris, cut back the banks and to dredge the bottom to keep the silted, sluggish river moving along. They incorporated as the Miles River Meadow Company in April 1880. It was regularly dredged and cleaned up until the early 1940s.

# Ice Industry

Another important seasonal industry for Hamilton was the ice trade. It is hard for us to imagine Chebacco Lake, Wenham Lake, Beck's Pond and other smaller bodies of water frozen at least ten inches deep by the middle of December, yet dated historic photos show this to be true.

When reading about the ice trade, it is generally recognized that Wenham Lake ice from Wenham, Massachusetts, a town adjacent to Hamilton, was the finest in this area. It is said that it was so clear and free of impurities that a newspaper could be read through two feet of its wondrous clarity. The ice trade flourished as a business in Hamilton, Wenham, Beverly and the surrounding area for over fifty years. For the purposes of this book, we will look at a little bit of general ice history but will predominately discuss the ice industry in and around Hamilton's Chebacco Lake, a 209-acre body of water that is approximately ten to twenty-two feet deep.

The word Chebacco is variously interpreted to mean "plentiful fishing" and "land where spirits dwell." A good catch of fish from the lake is still possible, and on some fall days, long ghostly threads of fog move about the woods and shores, so both names are good descriptions of the area.

Today, most people have ice easily available all year round from their refrigerator ice makers. But it was not always so easy to have cool drinks in summer or to prevent food spoilage from heat. American history shows that farmers cut ice as far back as the 1700s, preserved it in sawdust and used it to cool their milk and dairy products in the summer. Little icehouses were built, sometimes partially underground. Records show that George Washington was interested in keeping ice at Mount Vernon. At Monticello, Thomas Jefferson's home, there was ice available for use in the summer months.

It took the vision of a Boston man, Frederick Tudor (1783–1864), for ice to become a thriving industry. He became so successful at marketing it that at one time ice, packed in sawdust and rice chaff, was shipped via railroad from Hamilton and many other New England towns to Boston, and then was transferred into the holds of ships and exported to such far-off places as Rio de Janeiro, Brazil; Calcutta, India; Sidney, Australia; and Canton, China.

In the local area, too, there is evidence to show that long before ice was exported, local farmers cut and stored ice for their own use. Lawrence Lamson, the well-known former fire chief and Hamilton selectman, remembers his father damming up Black Brook in the back of his property (near Pingree School) and cutting ice on the pond that formed there for cooling their own milk and dairy products in the summer.

A lot of the local ice that was harvested stayed right in the vicinity. Much of the ice from Chebacco and Beck's was used locally, and the Hamilton Historical Society has several pictures of wagons and drivers delivering ice to Asbury Grove and to downtown businesses.

For local men, it was a welcome industry in the winter when farms were tranquil under snowy cover and the earning of a few extra dollars was welcome. The industry thrived so well that there are multipage marketing booklets in the Hamilton Historical Society promoting hundreds of tools for purchase and for use in different types of ice harvest. Man plows, horse plows, six-inch cutters, jack saws, pole grapples, ice adze, line markers, ice hooks, chisel bars, striking-up bars, needle bars and poling hooks are just a few of the diverse assortment of tools used.

C.W. Mears Icehouse on Chebacco Lake, 1929.

In *Crystal Blocks of Yankee Coldness* Philip Chadwick Foster Smith notes that usually by December, when the ice had become about ten inches thick, the men cleared the snow away and began to mark the area with two-inch grooves into a system of neat grids that were then sawn into blocks with horse-drawn saws. When the blocks were chiseled free by the men, they were pushed toward the icehouses for storage. They were stacked up with sawdust between them and straw on the top, and they could last for years without completely melting. Usually the icemen were able to obtain three harvests, the last being in March.

It was a cold and dangerous business. One slip into the water could cause a man to drown or disappear under the ice, not to be found until spring. Special harnesses were used for the horses so that they could break free if they fell in, but many did not survive a frigid tumble even if a difficult rescue could be managed. Some horses simply sank into the icy waters, never to be seen again.

There were several icehouses on Chebacco Lake. The Driver's Union Ice Co. (1877), near Echo Cove Road, had nine houses. There were

An assembly line of icehouse workers on Chebacco Lake.

Driver's Union Icehouse, circa 1900. The Boston and Maine Railroad is to the right.

Cutting ice on Chebacco Lake, circa 1920.

C.W. Mears (1893), Alvah P. Day and Bertram Mears Icehouses. On nearby Beck's Pond, Charles E. Whipple and his son Lester Whipple ran Whipple's Icehouse.

Driving by the lake today, it is difficult to imagine how vast these icehouses were, but some measured up to forty-eight thousand feet in length with storage for thousands and thousands of tons of ice. There were many outbuildings to accommodate this thriving production—boardinghouses, stables, homes, barns and sheds. The quantity of businesses that were occupied with ice harvesting points to it having been a lucrative enterprise for the time. C.W. Mears Company alone cut thirty-five thousand tons of ice each winter.

By 1850 a railroad had been built from Hamilton to Essex, and by 1872, a branch ran along a part of Hamilton's side of Chebacco Lake (Echo Cove), making it both easier to transport the ice and for workers to get to work. There was also a trolley that ran along Route 22. By 1920, modern refrigerators began replacing the messy iceboxes that had been in general domestic use and the ice industry began to wane.

Whipple Icehouses on Beck's Pond.

Woodbury Station of the branch line from Hamilton to Essex. This was the last stop for ice workers.

# Starling Burgess's First Flight

It would be remiss while on the subject of Chebacco Lake not to mention the first airplane flight in New England. In 1910, Norman Prince, a Harvard student at the time, invited his friends W. Starling Burgess, a boat builder and mathematical wizard, and Augustus M. Herring, an aeronautical engineer, to Hamilton to try out their newly built Herring/Burgess #1 biplane on Chebacco Lake. Prince's parents were traveling on the continent at the time.

The small plane was carted in pieces on a horse-drawn wagon, reassembled on the ice and on February 28, 1910, it took flight with Augustus M. Herring at the controls. The experimental plane was able to gain fifty feet of height.

According to an article by Alan Burke in the *Salem Evening News* on April 22, 2005, Burgess was able to sell the plane later for the astonishing sum (for the time) of $5,000. Word of his craftsmanship began to spread and he built some of the Wright brothers' planes. His technique was to wrap

A first flight on Chebacco Lake.

the wooden frame with sailcloth, and the planes he built were remarkably stable. He later pioneered the development of seaplanes, and during World War I, Burgess's factory supplied England, Canada and the United States with over a thousand airplanes.

Perhaps because of his habit of intense concentration on work, Burgess did not have a happy life. Infidelity and the death of his eldest son by drowning haunted him, but his daughter, also called Starling, became a noted children's author, writing under the name of Tasha Tudor.

W. Starling Burgess, a Marblehead native with a strangely prophetic bird name, made history on Chebacco Lake in Hamilton, Massachusetts.

# Hey, We Move Anything!

If a Hamilton resident wished to move his home from one lot to another today, it would perhaps cost more than the house is worth. All kinds of agencies would be called in—electric, water, sewer—and they would use cranes, bulldozers and flatbeds to facilitate the move. There would be a lot of energy and time spent procuring permits from various town departments.

Yet years ago, Hamilton folks moved many a home, barn, church or shed with efficiency and skill, using rather basic tools and gear, and it was usually accomplished without mishap. That is, except for one notable occurrence.

The equipment used to accomplish these extraordinary feats was simple: smooth logs, rollers, wheels, horses or oxen and wagons, a few willing men, a lot of interested onlookers to provide moral support and perhaps a comforting drink or two for the workers.

Sometimes parts of whole villages were moved and entire new neighborhoods were created, as was the case of the six homes on Mill Street previously located at the Willowdale Manufacturing Company. Purchased by George Adams in 1895, several wheels were attached to the corners of each house. They were pulled up the steep Highland Avenue hill past the Pingree estate by six strong horses sweating and straining their utmost, according to witnesses. Then the houses were set in place at their new location without much having gone awry. House lots of a quarter acre at the time were worth about $150. For the princely sum of $500 one could purchase over an acre of land in a prime location.

The houses at 648, 823 (recently a bed-and-breakfast) and 862 were moved back from the Bay Road. The Quarles House (1710) was moved from the corner of Essex and Miles River Road much farther down to 34 Miles River Road. All properties were substantial in size and would be deemed near impossible to move by today's standards.

The von Meyer House, located at approximately 710 to 800 Bay Road, the former home of George von Meyer, who served as ambassador to Russia under President Theodore Roosevelt and later was secretary of the navy during the term of President William Howard Taft, was a handsome estate surrounded by lush Italian gardens, attractive trees and shrubs of many varieties. In 1916, the house was cut into two pieces and raised to the top of the hill just behind it. Then, twenty years later, the house was again split in two, and one half was moved to a location farther down on the backside of the hill. This major move was all apparently carried out without mishap.

Where the Salem Five Bank is now located on Bay Road there was an impressive home with delicate gingerbread décor that was owned by Mr. Conrad, who was known to have been a very big man. Located in front of the house was a little store where he sold fish from a wooden cooler lined with zinc and filled with ice. It was said that his hands were so large that when he pulled a five- or six-pound cod or haddock from the cooler it looked like a minnow in his hands. The residence was moved in 1882 around the corner to Linden Street. It remains as a historical example of the lovely architecture of more leisurely times.

The Iron Rail house located on the corner of Grapevine and Essex Streets in Wenham was so large that it was cut up into three pieces and moved to Hamilton in 1976.

If a church in town were moved today, major newspaper articles would be written and it would disrupt traffic in the town for weeks. This was not the case in 1843. At that time, the Third Church of Christ, now the Congregational Church on Bay Road in Hamilton, was turned around so as to bring the front to face the street. The church then added twelve feet and was further expanded.

Mr. Lawrence Lamson, former selectman and fire chief, related a story of how he moved a garage from one side of town to his place of business on Willow Street using his old truck.

Mr. Robert A. McRae, also a former fire chief, has owned and operated a cobbler shop at 59 Willow Street for many years. His shop is the original South Schoolhouse (blackboards are still in evidence). It was also use as an Episcopal church for a while, and one of the old church doors still serves as a shelf in the shop. The building was later divided into three parts. Parts of two dwellings on Home Street are from the old schoolhouse. There are many other incidents of building relocation as Yankee thrift prevailed in Hamilton in regards to recycling property.

Once in a while things did not go so well. In 1889, George C. Creamer purchased from John R. Sargent the Hamilton House, which was a hotel and sometimes boardinghouse on Bay Road, with the intention to move it to another piece of land. For some reason, he chose the months of late December and early January to perform the feat.

New England weather plays a part in every endeavor of the region's inhabitants. Though the roads were frozen hard at first, changes in the weather caused them to become extremely muddy and the operation was bogged down. Men pushed and pulled and horses and oxen heaved and strained for hours, but to no avail. Quite suddenly, the house gave one great shudder and collapsed into itself—a total loss except for the salvage of lumber.

# Hamilton-Wenham Community House

In 1921 Mr. and Mrs. George and Emily Mandell had the community house building erected on a piece of property they had purchased on Bay Road. It is a remarkable memorial to their son Samuel and the other eight men from Hamilton and Wenham who volunteered to fight for the Allies in Europe before the official entry into World War I by the United States.

Sometimes referred to as the "Flying Galahads," the men were part of a group from America and Canada called the Lafayette Escadrille. Samuel Mandell, Augustus Gardner, Norman Prince, William Collins, William Taylor, Frank Nelson, Lester Hodgson and Reginald Young were the core group that fought against the Nazis, using the Sopwith and Spad single-engine fighter planes. This group later became the United States Aviation Service of France.

The Mandells gave the community house in a trust to the Hamilton House, an organization formed to be in charge of its upkeep and program planning. Though it was a memorial, the main purpose of the gift was for

The Hamilton-Wenham Community House.

educational and recreational use. Shortly thereafter, the Community Service of Hamilton and Wenham Inc. was organized.

At the front of the building there is a bronze statue by A.C. Ladd that was given to the Mandells as a surprise. The names of the brave men are memorialized by both this statue and a plaque.

Throughout the years, many have volunteered their services to raise money for the upkeep of the building and to assist in program and activity planning. C.G. Rice, a grandson of the Mandells, played an important leadership role in ensuring the mission and fulfilling the legacy of the Hamilton-Wenham Community House. Thousands of Hamilton and Wenham adults and children have been the benefactors of the Mandell family's generous gift.

# Mingo Corner

It surprises us now to think that Hamilton natives once owned slaves. In the early 1700s it was not unusual for those who could afford it. There were Native Americans as well as Africans who worked for their food in some form of slavery. There were also indentured servants, some of whom were criminals, sold to serve for whatever period of time their punishment was deemed reasonable. Other indentured servants were very poor people who agreed to a period of servitude in return for food, shelter and a pittance.

In 1755, according to Felt, there were sixty-two slaves above age sixteen in greater Ipswich, which at the time encompassed Hamilton and Essex. But in 1780, long before the Civil War, the state constitution declared that "all men are born free and equal." Slaves above the age of twenty-one could sue for emancipation and often were successful in obtaining freedom.

In Hamilton's vital statistics there are listed about twenty-five black men and women as residents in the town between 1714 and 1768: fourteen

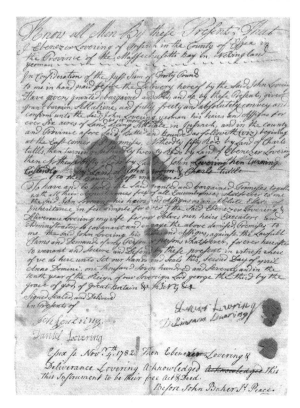

A slavery document.

males and twelve females. Both black and white people could be indentured. Indenture and purchase records show that one could work a certain amount of time and then become free, though for some, outright ownership of both them and their families was without end. One slave named Plato belonged to the Whipple family, and after many years of service, he was given his freedom and a piece of land later known as Plat's meadow. Recorded under the heading "Negro Deaths" in *Vital Records of Hamilton, Deaths*, is the following: "Plato, formerly a slave, born in Africa of a pious and excellent character, Dec. 24, 1799 age 107." He is also referred to in Felt's *History of Ipswich, Essex and Hamilton*.

In a short, two-page memoir by a grandchild of Manasseh Cutler, Eliza Poole Wheeler relates how excited she was to visit her grandfather and how, as they approached the house that was made lovely with various trees, vines and gardens, they passed the little cottage of the two Negro servants.

The Reverend Wigglesworth, several families of Whipples and the Brown, Dodge, Simon, Dane, Lovering and Thorn families are all listed as owning slaves. The corner of Asbury and Highland Streets was once known as Mingo's Corner after a black family that was owned by the Loverings, who lived there.

# School Days

In the early 1630s, during the time that our town was still known as the Hamlet and was still a part of Ipswich, there were no recorded schools in the district. But there may have been dame schools, small schools of three, four or five students taught by a woman. Other than that, children were taught basic letters and numbers at home if the parents were sufficiently literate to do so.

The early settlers knew that education enabled men to become leaders and that they had a better chance of becoming prosperous if they were literate. "Men" is the predominant word here, as few women were even taught to read. By 1636, there is evidence that a grammar school had brief success in Ipswich. In 1647, Massachusetts law required reading and writing schools for towns with over fifty families. By 1653, a real school building was constructed. The distance from Hamilton to the school probably limited the numbers of the Hamlet pupils able to attend as roads, transportation and weather were very unpredictable.

By 1730, a school was established in the Hamlet in the area near the present-day Congregational Church in Hamilton. At the time, this was the center of the town. Board and fuel were provided by the pupils for the master. A schoolmaster, Mr. Joseph Secomb, taught school there from the first of November to the last day of February.

As time went by, two terms of school were established. There were usually male teachers in the fall and winter when the students were predominantly boys. It was easier for boys to attend school in these seasons because during the planting and growing seasons of spring, summer and early fall, the boys were needed on home farms. Female teachers often taught during the spring and summer term.

Schools were overseen by a school committee of prominent townsmen, usually three in number, but more were added as more schools were established.

By 1793, when the Hamlet separated from the town of Ipswich and became Hamilton, there were four schools. The East School (1834) was located in the area of School Street across from the Legion. But by 1918, a more permanent building called the Adelaide Dodge Walsh School was built (the present-day American Legion Hall). The North School was located at the corner of Highland and Goodhue Streets but was later located roughly across from the present Hamilton-Wenham Regional/Miles River Middle School complex. The West School was located on Highland Street just beyond Winthrop Street. The Center School was located on Bay Road.

Each school was visited by one or several members of the school committee at the end of each term. Sometimes these visits were observed by the public. Random questioning was done to see if the pupils had attained a specific level of knowledge. Those schools that were considered to have attained a higher level of knowledge were a credit to the teachers. Latin and Greek were part of the curriculum because it was a prerequisite for Harvard College.

The school committee also closely monitored the lives of the teachers, and the hiring of teachers was often done with a minister's assistance to ensure honorable, principled and ethical temperament. Teachers must have attained a good education, use proper pronunciation and be correct in all manner of speech and deportment. A teacher must be able to enforce good behavior and to teach respect for others. Pupils who could not or would not learn or who disrupted the class were sent home permanently. It was the parents' responsibility to pay for each teacher's salary and to assist with fuel for both the school and teacher's quarters. Some teachers boarded with families.

East School, 1910.

South School, 1907.

North School, 1853.

Center School, circa 1891.

By 1869, the town of Hamilton began to pay for education and taxes were raised for that purpose. These small schools served quite well for many years. They were difficult to administrate, though, because of the separate regions, and after years of deliberation, the townspeople came to the conclusion that children would be better served if they were together in one school and that perhaps the expense would not be as great.

By the 1890s, a large building called the South School/Lamson School had been erected on the site that is now the Senior Housing Complex on Railroad Avenue. Later, the building was expanded and it was deemed sufficient for grades one through twelve. The first class to graduate from this school was the Class of 1911 and it consisted of two girls.

According to Hammond A. Young in his unpublished paper "Glimpses of the Hamilton Schools, 1636–1976," in 1931, because of the increasing population, a separate high school was built at the site of the present Hamilton-Wenham Library on land donated by Frederick Winthrop in memory of his wife. It later served as a junior high school when Hamilton and Wenham began to regionalize their school system in 1959. The Hamilton-Wenham Regional High School was built in 1961–62 on the former Weldon Estate on Bay Road.

# Sulky Racing

A sulky racetrack? In Hamilton? Yes, it was only a quarter mile long and it ran along the old Eastern Railroad, now a bridle path that runs from Walnut Street to Myopia.

There once was an organization called the Hamilton and Wenham Sulky Driving Club. The president of this organization was Norman J. Conrad.

Another name for sulky racing is "gig racing." According to Myrtle Conrad Bruce, "Every Wednesday the whole town closed down and headed for the track." In winter, the races were held on Idlewood Lake, now called Pleasant Pond. At age fifteen, Myrtle raced "Molly Coddle" on the dirt track, and "Oakland T" on the ice. She won the championship trotting cup for "Molly Coddle" in 1913.

Myrtle Conrad Bruce with "Molly Coddle."

A crowd turns out for the big race.

# Grass Rides

Located off Cutler Road, Grass Rides is the unique name given to the part of the Appleton Farms property that includes the remnants of approximately five miles of the woods-bordered carriage roads that crisscross over brooks, hills, water meadows and fields. Today, "the Rides" are used for recreational walking and are not generally available for horseback riding. They form a five-pointed star shape with each "ride" ending at a tall pinnacle that once was a part of Harvard University's college library. Altogether, there are four such pinnacles at Appleton Farms. They were given to the Appleton family in honor of its long association with Harvard.

# The Loud Cook

There are early books of cookery that, in addition to providing measurements and noting ingredients for recipes, admonished the homemaker to be prudent and to learn how to work quietly so as not to disturb the "master." Women were advised to shut drawers softly and to restrain from clattering pot lids. Objects necessary for cooking were to be put down quietly on a counter or tabletop. Thus, *all* domestic chores, especially cookery, would be serene and pleasant and harmony would prevail in the home. Whether she had ever heard these ancient etiquettes for housewifery is unknown, but one poor cook in our locale paid a terrible price for making too much noise.

It began on an estate on Asbury Street on the Topsfield line in November 1963. A doctor from Boston had called the police to report that one of his patients at that address was acting strangely and should be checked on. When the police responded, they began to search the estate and found nothing alarming. All appeared normal on the first floor. They checked the outside grounds and garage and still found nothing amiss. But there was an ominous and eerie silence.

Exploration of the second floor of the beautifully furnished mansion revealed a different story. Sprawled on the floor and strangled to death was the body of the cook.

Police, now wary and apprehensive, walked carefully from room to room, finding nothing unusual until they reached the library. There, they came upon a little man quietly absorbed in a book. The police asked the man what had happened and why he had done such a grievous thing? The man responded simply that the cook had aggravated him because she was making too much noise.

# The Vanished Diner

Hamilton once boasted its very own diner, whose specialty was a large and delectable hamburger for ten cents. The Hamilton Diner stood near where the Talbots store is now located on Depot Square and it did brisk business from 1932 until it closed its doors in 1958. It was mostly an eatery for men. Soon after, the diner was sold and moved to Route 114 behind Richardson's Dairy in Middleton, where it served for many years as a place for the dairy's workers to eat.

# PART III

# Quirky \ˈkwər-kē\ *adj.* Characters

*Having, exhibiting or suggesting unexpected features, qualities or character, all their own.*

# Gail Hamilton

One of the most idiosyncratic of characters that have lived in Hamilton was the Victorian author and poet Mary Abigail Dodge, better known by her pseudonym of Gail Hamilton. She used the pseudonym so that she could more freely express her opinions without censure, and opinionated she was! She was a woman ahead of her times, knowledgeable, well educated, well connected and quite certain that she was right at all times. She became well known in her lifetime both by her real name and by her adopted nom de plume; well enough so that there was a steamboat *Gail Hamilton* in Salem Harbor that ferried passengers to Baker's Island, and a similarly named boat operated at Centennial Grove in Essex.

Though she is classified mostly as an essayist and is considered to be a minor author in the time of flowery Victorian writing, her influence was strongly felt in Hamilton. Versatile in her work, she produced essays, sketches, biographies, novels, poetry, fiction, satires, brief articles on current topics and some juvenile work. She wrote remarkable, copious and detailed letters and the quotes in this chapter are from her letters and works, and from the book *Gail Hamilton 1833–1896* by Janice G. Pulsifer.

Her father James Brown Dodge was a prosperous farmer who married Hannah Stanwood in 1833. Gail was the youngest of seven children. She and her sister Hannah Augustus lived together on the Dodge property on Bay Road after their parents' deaths. Gail was small in stature and guarded her figure carefully, never weighing more than 115 or so pounds. A childhood accident with a fork had made her blind in one eye, but it was not really disfiguring, and pictures of Gail show a dignified young woman with a rather tart expression on her face. In later years, we see a white-haired woman with very sharp eyes and a look of shrewd but disdainful intelligence.

They were well-off for those times and could afford to travel and entertain as they wished. Gail taught school as a young woman, but left to devote her

Gail Hamilton, age twenty-one, in 1851.

life to writing and study. She attended readings, lectures, plays, concerts, operas and anything else that piqued her curiosity. She had an avid interest in metaphysical subjects.

We know a lot about what she thought and did by her abundant correspondence carried on with many of the famous people of her era. A friend of Nathaniel Hawthorne's, the author of *The Scarlet Letter,* and his wife Sophia Hawthorne, she visited them when they resided in Concord, Massachusetts. She went by horsecar and steam car to visit John Greenleaf Whittier, the renowned Quaker poet, abolitionist and her good friend, and he was often a guest at her home. Her letters to him are preserved in his archives. One written by Whittier, dated 1865 and addressed to her, is charming and shows the poet's Quaker manner of speech.

> *I was a little blue and out of sorts this morning but thy letter was just the tonic I needed. If anybody is out of sorts and unhappy I shall prescribe for him a course of thy letters. And now, God bless thee. Ever and truly thy fd. John G. Whittier.*

Louis Agassiz, Julia Ward Howe, Lowell, Holmes, Henry James and Longfellow were Gail's colleagues and frequent correspondents. She wrote to President Abraham Lincoln to encourage him when he was reelected for a second term.

In 1858, she went to live in Washington with the Gamaliel Bailey family. This was just for the wintertime, as she usually returned to Hamilton for the summer. Gamaliel Bailey was the editor of the *National Era*, an antislavery tabloid, and he was a stanch antislavery agitator. It was during this time of war that Gail contributed many articles to the publication. Later, she went to live with the family of James G. Blaine, who was then Speaker of the House of Representatives and also served as secretary of state under Presidents Garfield and Harrison. His wife Harriet Stanwood was Gail's own cousin. At this time, Gail became very interested in political discussion and wrote letter after letter to the newspapers. It is reported that she was of great assistance to Mr. Blaine prior to the time he published his book, *Twenty Years in Congress.*

While she was living with the Blaines, she conducted a Bible class that was sponsored by the president and vice-president of the United States in which she declared "all religions were amiably represented." When the notes for these classes were published, she made enough money to repaint her home in Hamilton, restore the barn, install a windmill to pump water and make other improvements. These publications seemed to give her a little élan in regards to the subject of religion, because later, many a clergyman was called to task for various parts of a sermon when she did not agree with particular points, whether they were preaching from the local Congregational pulpit or in a Washington church. Throughout her life, morality and religion in relationship to her life and the lives of others continued to be her favorite subjects.

We learn some interesting things about Gail Hamilton from her writing. Peddlers came to her door, one in a long, high, red cart to buy rags and paper, another a German with a pack on his back and one a clerical-looking man with a box of soap as a present. Someone once peered in her parlor window and had to be sent off by a summoned townsman who escorted the voyeur out of town on the next train. There is also a tale of a woman suffragist who came to her door.

Gail's sour comments on her maids show a lot of prejudice and make one wonder how difficult it must have been to work for her. The poor maids seemed to come and go in brisk progression. She referred to them in a derogatory way as the "Celtic handmaids," and though Irish maids were sought after because they were inexpensive and plentiful, she had no patience with them. She wrote:

*Mary is a treasure but she can't make bread, Mother Patrick, a Scotchwoman who boils onions with the potatoes has seasons of withdrawing from the world.*

Gail suspected that Mother Patrick was either smoking or tippling. Within two weeks, the maid had left with all her belongings. According to Gail:

*I gave her five dollars, a Boston ticket, her fare to the station, a flannel petticoat, and a package of paper and envelopes and she departed in peace, as dirty a heap of good nature as I ever saw and if I ever get the flavor of onions out of the dishes I will be glad.*

There was also a woman from Prince Edward Island who was dismissed for inhospitality and brutal manners. Another poor woman called Wendell "left us very suddenly on one night's notice." Of a little Nova Scotia maid, Gail said:

*She is such a pretty, neat, well-mannered girl that I want her well mannered, but I prefer that she should remain un-manned at present.*

But this poor little maid did not last very long either.

In one notable instance Gail reported that new carpet treads were being put on the stairs, and a child who belonged to a maid was interested in the tacks and hammer. She warned him away, but when he did not heed her words, Gail tapped his fingers smartly with her "little" hammer.

Though acerbic, she could be kind when she was so inclined. On one occasion, she bought three pounds of candy and treated the children as they came home from school.

Some of her observations on things are cutting yet comical. She was pleased with the attention of men, stating, "I have friends on every side who delight in me, men and women who come to me for joy and solace and strength." Yet she was happy to refuse all proposals and made many comments on the marital state:

*I am independent, and every man is my humble servant. If I were married, I should be dependent upon the caprices of one. An unmarried woman has an immense advantage over married women—I like women. In fact I esteem them very highly, but I bag higher game when I can. Women do well to fall back upon, but for first choice give me a brace of bearded men.*

One characteristic of Gail's that carried through to old age was her Yankee thrift. She could not resist making use of blank paper, and she was

> known to write her essays etc. on ruled tablets, and on the back of instruction sheets for erecting lightening conductors and on the back of an abandoned agreement with her publishers Harper and Brothers.

Though charitable, she was sometimes criticized for her elitist ways. In some circles she was well known and admired for her literary achievements, but she was disparaged in others. Always in elegant attire as a young woman, in later years she could be seen about town, in outdated, overworn finery as her frugality and thrift became parsimonious and would not allow for the disposal of what was still a bit useful.

At the time of her death in August 1896, the newspapers were full of praise for this Victorian writer, but some could not refrain from a few less favorable comments.

Some of her publications were: *Country living and Country Thinking*, *Gala Days*, *Wool Gathering*, *Summer Rest*, *Woman's Wrongs*, *A Counter-Irritant*, *A Battle of the Books*, *First Love is Best* and *What Think Ye of Christ?*

There is a lovely stained-glass window in the First Congregational Church given in her memory by her sister Augusta. Her grave in the Hamilton Cemetery reads: "Death is but the unfolding of a higher life."

# Colonel Robert Dodge

Colonel Robert Dodge, a famous Hamilton Patriot, was not known for his idiosyncrasies, but for his extraordinary kindness, and this by itself makes him a singular public figure of his time.

One of the six children of his hardworking parents, Isaac and Lois Dodge, he was born in 1743 and lived for eighty years. When he was only twenty-two, he married Mary Boardman, a young woman from nearby Ipswich. They lived with his father and stepmother at the family farm off of Bay Road, now the Myopia Hunt Club.

When he was thirty-one years old, he was planting barley in an upper field when the alarm call came on April 19, 1775. His rank then was first lieutenant, and he served under Captain Elisha Whitney (who was then Hamilton's physician). Their orders were to ride to Milton, Massachusetts, to help rout the English. Manasseh Cutler, the pastor from the Congregational Church, met with the company before it set off.

Many years later, his grandchildren told a story of their grandmother's great distress at his departure. Apparently the distant sound of cannons could be heard even on the farm. The next morning, when she could stand the uncertainty no longer, she took a horse and chaise and drove off by herself to Charlestown to see what was going on. Nothing else is known of this little tale, but apparently she eventually returned and so did he. Today, this would probably be comparable to the wife of one of our soldiers fighting in Iraq taking a plane to Baghdad, then driving a tank to check things out in the area of major conflict. She is described as a "rather portly woman, with a fine presence and manners" but with very strong lungs. All through the time of her husband's absence, the well-managed farm suffered no losses.

By the time the war ended, Dodge had been commissioned colonel. He participated in at least twenty-three battles, including Dorchester Heights and Bunker Hill, and served in places as far away as New York and Trenton.

He is said to have become so upset at the sight of Hessian soldiers, the mercenaries of that time, that he would rush at them with his sword in one hand and his hat in the other, yelling, "Rush on ye devils, rush on ye devils."

After the conflict ended, Mary and Robert went on to have eight sons and two daughters, but only six sons lived to adulthood.

His family describes him as a man with a strong, hearty build and a broad, kindly face. Though he had little formal education, he was naturally perceptive and well suited for maintaining and improving the farm that he had inherited from his father Isaac. It was a large piece of property, the homestead lot of eighty-three acres in the Hamlet, thirty acres in Beverly, forty-three acres in Wenham and land in the great Wenham swamp. In 1772, he built a new farmhouse in the exact same location as the old one.

In 1866, the farm was sold to John Gibney, a Salem merchant. Though Gibney ran the farm for a few years, there is a picture that shows the farm when it was being rented out as the clubhouse for the Myopia Hunt Club. In 1891, the club purchased the property.

During Robert Dodge's ownership, the farmland yielded crops of barley, rye, Indian corn, potatoes and flax, as well as various small vegetable crops. In the meadows and barns were cows, oxen, sheep and pigs. Unusual for the times, Robert led the way for his neighbors in the cultivation of trees.

This was the home of Colonel Robert Dodge in 1772. Photo circa 1884.

Reportedly he had nearly four thousand trees planted on some of his acreage, including walnuts, white oaks, shagbark hickory, chestnuts, elms and white ash.

Around 1818 there was an advertisement in the local newspaper for elm trees that were to be put into the grounds of the Salem Common to substitute for the Lombardy poplars that were then in place. About that time Robert was honored by the Massachusetts Society for Promoting Agriculture, receiving an award of $100.

According to research, (*Robert Dodge, Hamilton's Minute Man*, by Janice G. Pulsifer) he was active in all parish affairs, becoming a collector of rate, an assessor, a moderator and a representative in the Massachusetts General Court. He considered Manasseh Cutler, the minister of the Congregational Church, to be one of his dearest friends. Documents show that the two families spent time together. Cutler and Dodge both worked on the committee that separated the Hamlet from Ipswich in 1793. Although he was of kindly demeanor, the colonel occasionally was not able to rein in his temper and church records of the time show that he was "disciplined," sometimes twice a year. When a particularly thorny dispute arose between the colonel and his neighbor John Wittredge, the minister offered to quell the fire by proposing to pray with him. "What shall I pray for," the minister asked the fiery Dodge. Never admitting wrong, Robert Dodge replied, "Well, pray for Mr. Wittredge, and when you are through with that I'll give you some others to pray for!"

Generally, though, Robert Dodge was a man of genial temperament, in comfortable means and happy with his family. But he did something that was unusual for the time. He loaned out money to friends, neighbors and various folk without equity or surety simply to help people out. He offered hospitality and assistance whenever he could. In one instance, a young man newly arrived from Ireland boarded with the Dodge family. The man taught school for a while at one of the small local schools before moving to Newburyport to become master of the grammar school there. Later, he became a celebrated mathematician. His book, *A New System of Mercantile Arithmetic, Adapted to the Commerce of the United States and Foreign Relations*, was an important work of the time.

There is no evidence to show that Robert Dodge ever suffered loss from his generosity and kindness.

# Samuel Wigglesworth

Samuel Wigglesworth was born on February 4, 1688, in Malden, Massachusetts, and was the sixth child and only son of Reverend Michael Wigglesworth and Martha Mudge. He was only two years old when his mother died and his father married for the third time.

After the usual private tutoring of the time, Samuel was sent to Harvard for his education. Harvard at the time was a very strict college and graduated many ministers, but its chief undertaking was to provide its graduates with a liberal education.

Samuel received a scholarship. Though small in build and short in stature, he had a fiery temper, and while at college he became "involved in one of the worst disorders of his college generation." At the time, fines were charged for offenses such as absence from prayer meetings, walking on Sunday, gambling for money, playing cards, breaking down doors, picking locks or frequenting forbidden houses. Whatever happened, he had to pay a fine of one pound, a substantial sum at the time as it was worth one year of boarding. This may have caused him to believe that he was not fit for the ministry. Shortly afterward, in 1709, he apprenticed himself to a Doctor Greaves to study medicine, and by 1710, he had come to the Hamlet to begin his practice as a physician. Samuel practiced dentistry, administering poultices, using common herbs for healing and bleeding when necessary. He also served as an apothecary. In general, his fee was about sixpence.

After a year or so, he returned to Boston to study for the ministry. On October 12, 1714, he was elected minister at the parish meeting, and on October 27, 1714, he was ordained.

One of the people attending the ordination was Samuel Sewall, the only judge of the Salem witch trials who later formally repented and did penance by wearing a hair shirt for the rest of his life. Also in attendance were the Reverend Mr. Gerrish of Wenham and the Reverend Mr. John Wise of Chebacco Parish (Essex).

Samuel's first salary was sixty pounds, with part of it in grain and wood. He received one and a half acres of land adjacent to the meetinghouse on which to build his home.

We now associate houses of this era with rather plain designs. But olive green, pumpkin yellow, Indian red and gray were the most common colors for homes at this time, for those who could afford paint. The Wigglesworth House, with many changes, is now a private residence next to the First Congregation Church in Hamilton.

Known for his integrity and principles, Samuel was much loved at the Hamlet. His own notes show that he prepared many sermons on various topics and that sometimes he would repeat the same sermon with a new introduction or ending. One sermon, preached on New Year's Day, would make even the most derelict of souls repent. "Behold I will cast thee from off the earth; this year thou shalt die, because thou hast taught rebellion against the Lord" (Jeremiah 28:16). He died at age eighty, after ministering for fifty-four years.

Samuel's remarkable character is shown in a quote from Gail Hamilton's book *X-Rays*. When he was quite elderly, he was seen setting out a new apple seedling. One of his parishioners came along and, seeing him on his knees, said, "Sir, you cannot expect to reap any fruit from your labor."

"No," he replied. "I am only paying a debt."

# Manasseh Cutler

The second minister of the Hamlet, Manasseh Cutler, was born in Killington, Connecticut, in 1744, and was the eldest son of Susanna (Clark) and Hezekiah Cutler, an influential farmer. Manasseh was educated at Yale in 1768. He read law, passed the bar and administered a few cases, but then he became a ship chandler because he felt that the business was very lucrative. In 1766 he met and married Mary (Polly) Balch. He later studied theology with his father-in-law, Reverend Balch, and shortly thereafter received his license to preach. He was asked to preach at the Hamlet for a few months after the death of the Reverend Samuel Wigglesworth and the congregation liked him. On September 11, 1771, he was ordained and began his tenure at the First Congregational Church.

Dr. Manasseh
Cutler, 1743–1823.

He purchased the home of Reverend Wigglesworth from his widow. The Hamlet was fortunate in its choice of Dr. Cutler. Always very correct and dapper in his dress, he was a man of true intellect with a sharp and inquisitive mind. He studied medicine, botany and astronomy. He is considered to be a pioneer of botanical science. He loved outdoor adventure and was one of a party of six considered to be the first white men to climb Mount Washington in New Hampshire.

As a member of the American Academy, Manasseh wrote articles on all kinds of subjects: eclipses, meteorology and natural history. He was an honorary member of the Philadelphia Linnaean Society, a member of the Massachusetts Agricultural and Historical Society and a member of the American Antiquarian Society.

When the news of the British marching on Concord was received, he addressed the company of men from Hamilton who were going out to fight and later went out to see for himself how things were going. In 1776, toward the end of the Revolutionary War, he received the commission of chaplain.

Though the Revolutionary War was successful, the nation had a huge war debt that needed to be paid. At the same time, there was little revenue coming in and the nation was in such disarray that there was no one in charge who seemed able to manage the problem. Janice G. Pulsifer, in her book *Cutlers of Hamilton*, wrote:

> *The Hamlet, full of prosperous farmers, suggested that the rich lands northwest of the Ohio River, chiefly belonging to the states, should be sold. The soldiers, to whom a large part of the debt was due, were willing to take the land as payment if the government would give them a good title and the States were willing to surrender their claim to the general government and this would ease the financial strain.*

The Hamlet's minister Manasseh Cutler was chosen to be in charge when the Ohio Company of Associates was formed to negotiate the procurement of 1.5 million acres of land and its settlement. He went to Congress and asked for an ordinance for the government of the territories, claiming that "if families ventured out on this enterprise, we must know beforehand what kind of foundation we will build on." He was a key figure in getting the Ordinance of 1787 passed, setting up the whole framework for the opening of the Northwest Territories. The ordinance included freedom of religion, provision for education of children and most important and far-seeing for the time, the exclusion of slavery.

Cutler came back home and without delay ordered that a large canvass-covered wagon be built. By December 3, 1787, under the command of

Major Haffield White, a group of forty-five men set off from in front of the parsonage to settle the new country. The wagon had painted on its side the phrase "Ohio for Marietta on the Muskingum." For months afterward, the Reverend Manasseh Cutler's home and courtyard were occupied by people and wagon trains preparing to leave for the Ohio.

This activity suited the vigorous minister, and the following summer he drove himself in a sulky to the new settlement to see how his men were faring. After arriving in Marietta, he was still energetic enough to preach to the people on Sunday and later to venture out and look over interesting landscape features.

It was Manasseh Cutler who led the movement to become incorporated as a separate town from Ipswich on June 21, 1793. There was opposition, but the town of Ipswich accepted with reluctance a compensation of a little over £908 in silver coins delivered in person by Dr. Cutler and his friend Colonel Robert Dodge to Ipswich's town treasurer.

Dr. Cutler went on to serve as a member of the Seventh and Eighth Congresses and was honored and admired by all. He was in his fifty-second year as a minister of the Hamilton Congregational Church when he passed away at age eighty-two, leaving behind an important intellectual legacy to Hamilton and to the country.

# Joseph B. Felt

The third minister of the First Congregational Church, Joseph B. Felt (1789–1869), served the parish for only nine years. He had a rather austere personality that was in sharp contrast to Cutler's bonhomie, and he was judged rather unfairly. He suffered from asthma, which made it difficult for him to preach and carry on his work. Yet he left us a distinctive legacy. Much of what we know of Essex County's history is due to his intellect and curiosity.

Felt authored the *History of Ipswich, Essex and Hamilton* (1833), an invaluable source for historians, and the *Annals of Salem* (1827). Felt's *History of Massachusetts Currency* (1839), a second *Annals of Salem* (1849) and the *Genealogical Items for Gloucester and Lynn* (1850) are all distinctive for their scholarship, as are papers he wrote on well-known citizens of the time.

He became the Massachusetts Historical Society's librarian and later served as president of the New England Historic Genealogical Society. Though his service at the First Congregational Church in Hamilton was brief in comparison to the other ministers, his interest in the Essex County area has been a remarkable benefit to Hamilton.

# George L. von Meyer

Although George L. von Meyer was not a native, he became a renowned citizen in Hamilton. His father was a German immigrant who entered the country through New York City. Later, George L. von Meyer Sr. moved to Boston and married into society that enabled him to live in comfortable circumstances. He educated his three children well, and as the eldest, George graduated from Harvard at the age of twenty-one. He was as successful as his father socially, and in a short while he controlled a large amount of the banking and commercial world in northeastern Massachusetts. He married socially prominent Marion Appleton in 1885 and they bought a home in Hamilton.

George was likable, shrewd and keen, with sharp business expertise and good social skills. He had the drive often seen in immigrants and their children. An entry in his diary indicates how important it was to him to make something of his life.

A staunch Republican, he began his political career in Boston, first as a member of the city counsel and then in the Massachusetts legislature, becoming Speaker of the House in 1894. He was appointed ambassador to Italy in early 1900 by President McKinley. Under President Roosevelt, he served as ambassador to Russia. A few years later, he became postmaster general.

George loved everything Italian and ordered that ornate Italian gardens be built at his home with creative stonework, artistic décor and the imaginative statuary of an Italian villa. All kinds of trees and shrubs became part of the elaborate landscape. Two little girls, Julia and Alice, and a son George Jr. were born to George and Marion in this country paradise. Because of the abundance of fine maple trees, the estate was called Rock Maple Farm. (Now located along Meyer Lane, Meyer Road and Rock Maple Avenue.)

One can imagine how ordinary Hamilton farmers responded to this amazing luxury. Many of the employees at the residence were local folk, and the resplendence of the von Meyers was part of local gossip. In spite of all the grandeur and opulence, there is evidence that accord was not always present. In 1916, two years before von Meyer's death, the house was split in two and moved back from the road and farther up the hill. Later it was split in two again, and this time one half was moved back down to the other side of the hill.

In 1998, one part of this estate became embroiled in a controversy that ended in a virtual siege involving much of the media and many law enforcement officers. John Sweeney had inherited one half of the houses and the other half had been sold to non-family members. In August 1987 he had secured a loan from the Comfed Savings Bank of Lowell for the purpose of financing a fourteen-lot subdivision of the estate.

After a long series of lawsuits, bad luck and unfortunate events, federal marshals arrested him in his home. Later, as reported in the *Salem Evening News* of March 3, 1998, he stated that "they can take our property, they can take our possessions, but they can't and will never take our spirit."

# Bradley Palmer

There are those who still remember Mr. Bradley Palmer (1866–1946) galloping about his estate on a dashing steed, pipe clenched tight in his teeth with a cigar standing upright in the bowl of a pipe, his sleek hound Badger running alongside. Why he smoked his beloved cigars in this manner, no one seems to know.

Bradley Palmer's life is somewhat obscure and apparently he wanted it that way. He was probably considered an eligible bachelor at the time, but he never married and there are no romantic interests recorded.

According to Steve Landwehr in his article "Bradley Palmer, Man of Mystery" in the *Salem Evening News* on July 17, 1999, Palmer was born in Wilkes-Barre, Pennsylvania, and later graduated from Philips Exeter Academy and Harvard. After being admitted to the Massachusetts Bar, he joined the law firm of Storey and Thorndike. During World War I, he was appointed as a United States representative and assisted in the negotiation of the Treaty of Versailles.

Bradley Palmer in 1888.

His passions were horses, cigars, horticulture, acquiring land and building houses on his estate. In total, he purchased over five square miles of property in Hamilton, Topsfield and Ipswich. The area of Bradley Palmer Park that he donated is roughly 750 acres. He gave to the people of Massachusetts 2,400 acres to be used as a state forest and wildlife sanctuary. The town of Topsfield received a gift of 190 acres of land.

Lawrence Lamson, former Hamilton selectman and fire chief, remembers seeing Mr. Palmer often when he was a child. Palmer would ride down to the road of his home and say to his father, "Well, Mr. Lamson, what can I buy from you today?" Mr. Palmer acquired much of his acreage in this way, by asking farmers if they were willing to sell and reportedly paying a fair rate.

He began acquiring land about 1891. The Joseph Lamson Farm (Joseph was a relative of Lawrence Lamson) was purchased in 1898, and it comprised 757 acres. Mr. Palmer lived there for a while when his mansion was being built. The road that ran through the area at the time was changed and straightened to its present design because Palmer was annoyed that traffic passed too closely to the mansion site. He offered to build a new bridge over the Ipswich River and the road was rerouted to please him. The bridge, which for many years was just a few planks laid over the water, was redesigned and reinforced. At one time Palmer ordered a whole freight car full of specially imported azaleas, rhododendron and laurel. These same plantings can still be enjoyed each spring on several parts of the properties of Bradley Palmer State Park and Willowdale.

There were more than thirty buildings on the estate originally, though many fell to ruin and have since been torn down. Master stonemasons hired from Italy crafted the stone buildings from the numerous stone walls of the Lamson properties. One interesting building still standing at one of the entrances to the park is a rather ornate stone and clapboard henhouse.

The main house is a majestic Tudor revival fieldstone mansion. Recently restored at the cost of approximately $1.5 million, it contains eight guest rooms, a parlor, a great room, a dining room and a library.

When the mansion was occupied by Palmer, he is reported to have been a gracious host who entertained often. The Prince of Wales rode with him on his estate, and President William Taft was an occasional visitor.

Palmer's generosity in donating immense tracts of land that he helped to preserve and protect are a gift that will be enjoyed forever by all, but it is for his quirky smoking of an upright cigar in a pipe and his nearly reckless horsemanship that older folks in Hamilton remember him.

# General George S. Patton Jr.

There are two pillars, French Memorial Road markers, located at the Bay Road entrance to Patton Park that commemorate General George S. Patton Jr. and his Third United States Army's assistance in liberating the towns of Avranches and Le Harve during World War II. They were sent by the French as a grateful tribute to Patton and his men. A special dedication ceremony took place at the park on April 15, 1953, shortly after they were put in place.

Most certainly General George S. Patton Jr. will forever be one of Hamilton's greatest heroes and most unusual characters. He was born on November 11, 1885, in San Gabriel, California. In 1910, a year after he graduated from the United States Military Academy at West Point, he married Beatrice Banning Ayer, a native of Boston and Prides Crossing, Massachusetts. Military life necessitated that they travel and live all over the world, but around 1928 they had purchased the farm "Green Meadows" in Hamilton and occasionally spent time there.

General George S. Patton Jr.

Patton's strong personality, purpose and resolve to succeed were rewarded by a steady rise in rank and reputation. He served in World War I as part of General Pershing's staff and was wounded in 1918. He then returned to the United States, where he continued to distinguish himself. By 1941, he was commanding officer of the Second Armored Division at Fort Benning, Georgia. In 1943, he became commanding general of the Western Task Force and was in charge of ground forces in Tunisia. During World War II he became the commanding general of the United States Third Army. General Patton commanded the respect of his men and he had a reputation as a tough general who got things done. By 1945, the United States occupied Germany and Patton was in command of the Fifteenth Army. There are many historians who believe that without Patton's expertise World War II might have had a very different outcome.

Patton was legendary for his military effort, yet he had a gentle side too. He is recognized as a hero for the World War II rescue of the famed Royal Lipizzaner stallions. During his last visit to Hamilton, Massachusetts, in June 1945, General George Patton was greeted as a returning hero by cheering crowds that had turned out to meet him at a ceremony at the Hamilton High School grounds. Patton was a figure larger than life. Hilda Cummings, who was visiting her sister in Asbury Grove at the time, brought her little girl Elaine to the ceremony. As everyone lined up to shake the general's hand, his salty language peppered some of the conversation being broadcast by a mike. At each exclamation, Hilda put her hands over her daughter's ears. When she finally reached the general, the little four-year-old put out her left hand to shake the renowned general's hand. He looked at her kindly and then took her small hand in his large one and said, "This is the right one little girl."

He received numerous awards, including the Order of the British Empire, the Distinguished Service Cross, the Bronze Star, the Purple Heart and a Victory Medal with four stars to name just a few.

On December 21, 1945, General Patton died of complications resulting from an automobile accident, just a few days before he was scheduled to return home to the United States. He is buried in the U.S. Army cemetery at Luxembourg.

Mrs. Beatrice Patton lived on at Green Meadows for many years after the general's death. In 1953, while out riding to hounds, she died of a heart attack.

Patton's son, Major General George Smith Patton, who was the tenth member of his family of military leaders, was a student at West Point during World War II. After an illustrious career, he retired to Green Meadows with his wife Joanne (Holden) Patton. They raised five children. They have generously provided numerous festivities at the farm for the public. Green Meadows is considered one of the finest organic farms in the area.

# Helen Frick
## *The Iron Rail*

The Iron Rail house, built about 1700, was so named because in its early days it boasted of a distinctive iron rail around it. The iron was used for the war effort during World War II. Though this house was originally in Wenham and plays an important role in Wenham's history, there is a Hamilton connection to it and to Helen Frick, daughter of Henry Clay Frick, of Prides Crossing in Beverly Farms. Henry had made millions in the steel industry. Around 1909, he purchased the property for her so that she could continue her charitable work.

Helen had been brought up in great luxury, but she was a witness to the sufferings of an older sister who was ill for many years. The little girl had ingested a small black-headed pin when she was very young, and as a result, she was weak, unable to eat and suffered from severe pain. In the days before X-rays, no one knew what was wrong with her and no medical help relieved her suffering. Helen, the empathetic younger sister, was called into her room often to entertain her sister. Her sister's death was a traumatic event for Helen and all the family.

Even as a young woman, Helen had great empathy for those who were less fortunate than herself. She witnessed the hard, grueling lives of the young girls, often only twelve to fourteen years old, who worked in the mills of Haverhill, Lawrence, Lowell, New York City and other localities. They toiled long hours at shifts that generally ran from 6:00 a.m. to 6:00 p.m. with a half day on Saturdays. The average wages were often less than five to twelve dollars per week. Helen wanted to do something for these girls that would make their lives easier and more enjoyable. She decided on a sort of home, where young women could vacation for a week or so during the spring and summer months. She staffed it with a cook, a gardener to care for the grounds and a director for the girls.

A social worker from the City Missionary Society in Boston, Ellen R. Boyd, was hired to assist Helen, and by the summer of 1910 they had chosen a few girls to begin the program.

The girls came by train and trolley with expenses paid by Helen. They were given a room and were cared for, served nutritious meals and provided with recreational activities and entertainment. Mary Anne Burridge, co-curator of the Hamilton Historical Society, recalls seeing the girls dressed in their Sunday best on summer weekends, being driven around in a large wagon to church or to Centennial Grove to enjoy a day of picnicking and boating.

Eventually, cottages were built around the property and the girls managed their own housekeeping. A large gymnasium was built to provide the girls with exercise and physical activities. When Miss Boyd's mother became ill, Helen had a home called Fairhaven built on the property to house them both.

By 1934, things had changed and the property was incorporated as the Iron Rail Vacation Homes. Later, it was donated to the Girls Club of America, and in 1974 it was purchased by the town of Wenham.

In the book *Wenham in Pictures and Prose* it is reported that letters have survived from some of the young women who were fortunate enough to benefit from Miss Frick's benevolence. In them, the girls express their happiness in meeting her, document her kindness to them and convey how much the retreat meant to them and what effect her compassion had on their lives.

# Lady Nancy Astor/ Nancy's Corner

At the junction of Highland Street and Cutler Road, originally known as Farms Road, there was once an old beamed and wood-pegged barn that was lost in a mysterious fire. This spot is traditionally known as Nancy's Corner because Lady Nancy Astor (1879–1964) fell off her horse here long ago. She is remembered in her youth as a charming, beautiful, fiery redhead.

Lady Nancy Astor was born in Virginia and married Robert Gould Shaw II, who built a home for her in Hamilton. Later she divorced him, traveled to England and married Waldorf Astor. The Astor Home at Cliveden, Buckinghamshire, England, became the scene of many social and political gatherings.

With little formal education, she went on to take a seat in the House of Commons in England (1919) and was the first woman ever to do so. She was a strong advocate for temperance and social reform, and she would fight hard for what she believed, but she did not like to be crossed. There are many stories of her acerbic wit, sharp sayings and feisty retorts.

Miss Nancy Shaw (later Lady Astor) at Legion Show.

Tales of the time claim that she was upset when Winston Churchill ignored her during the first few months of her term. When confronted, he replied that he was trying to ignore her because when she took her seat in the House of Commons, a traditional male bastion, he "felt as if a woman had come into [his] bathroom and [he] had only a sponge with which to defend [himself]."

She had a way with words and her pithy comments were called "Astorism" by the British. One infamous remark was: "We women do not ask for superiority, we have always had that. We ask for equality!"

Her most famous quote, as documented in the May 3, 1964 *Boston Sunday Herald*, came about when she was angered by Winston Churchill:

> *Lady Astor: "If you were my husband I'd poison your tea!"*
> *Winston Churchill: "Lady if I were your husband I'd drink it!"*

# Harrie Durham

There are many old-timers in Hamilton who still recall an unusual character by the name of Harrie M. Durham, who wandered about the streets of Hamilton wearing an odoriferous fur coat whatever the season. Though his name is written Harry in many places, his real name was Harrie. It was thought that he had attained a reasonable education at some time, but in his middle and later years his actions were such that they provided a lot of fodder for Hamiltonian's gossip.

He was sometimes referred to as the "Mayor of Asbury Grove," and the *Beverly Evening Times* reported on July 27, 1915:

> *Mingo Park, Highland Avenue near Asbury Grove has been surveyed and lots staked out are for sale by Harrie M. Durham, Asbury Grove, where plans can be seen and lots will be shown those who wish to buy.*

Earlier in the same year, on June 14, the *Beverly Evening Times* had reported in the Asbury Grove news section:

Harrie (often spelled Harry) in front of his house.

*A great crowd is expected here on the 17th, everything is ready to engage the visitors and Harrie Durham the photographer, is ready to take the pictures of those who are out for a day's outing.*

Harrie at one time was a photographer, and a fairly good one, but as the years went by he forgot that film was needed to produce pictures, and many folks stood or sat in tedious posing sessions that produced nothing.

At a time when it was uncommon in the region, Harrie was constantly advertising for a wife. One of the stories told is that of a young woman arriving on the Boston train at the Hamilton–Wenham Depot with a young child in tow. She approached a police officer on duty in the downtown area and inquired as to the whereabouts of Harrie, claiming she had come to marry him. The police officer enlightened her a bit about Harrie's circumstances, and she thanked him politely and waited for the return train into the big city.

He must have been successful in his courtships, though, because in his fourth venture into matrimony, Harrie, then age seventy, married Mary E. Sherry of Watertown, Massachusetts. After a welcome home celebration

This family stayed at Asbury Grove for many summers, coming from Chelsea in June and staying until September. *Harrie Durham photo.*

Harrie settled into his cottage with his new bride and the legions of cats that roamed into and about his home.

The multiple cats' situation went on for many years and there are a variety of felines in Hamilton that can boast the same genealogical line as Harrie's infamous cats.

Another story told by Hamilton folks is how Harrie would come downtown to shop wearing his long fur coat, no matter what the season, and carrying a bucket to hold whatever he planned to purchased. One day a chauffeur-driven limousine from one of the estates in Hamilton was parked outside Connolly's Drugstore and, recognizing that it was going his way and feeling a bit tired, Harrie entered the vehicle and made himself comfortable. Upon returning, the driver immediately noticed an odd smell and he was none too pleased to find Harrie lounging in the backseat. Harrie was not about to move, however, and he got the ride he wanted that day and many other times as well.

On a sad note, years later Harrie's home burned to the ground in a mysterious fire.

# Walter

Not all of Hamilton's interesting characters were human. There was at least one famous canine character that must be remarked upon.

We do not see dogs roaming the streets in Hamilton because of the strict leash law that is now in effect. But at one time there were many dogs roaming about, socializing, getting into fights, checking out people's rubbish and in general making themselves known.

Family dogs were as well recognized as the children who belonged to an assortment of addresses in each neighborhood. Children walked to school and their dogs often accompanied them, ending up in midmorning at the schoolyard, meeting, mixing, socializing, sniffing, snuffling, messing, wrestling, checking each other out, playing "king of the mountain" and in general causing a lot of exciting commotion and mayhem to the despair of principals and teachers. Several calls to parents to "come get your dog" were not unusual from the school secretaries on any given morning. Some canines arrived at the back doors of restaurants for their daily (stolen or otherwise) treats and took their naps in sunny doorways. They went undisturbed, and if they ambled too slowly across busy streets or the railroad crossings, cars simply waited and the train conductor might just give one little toot to hurry things along.

Most of these noble canines have trotted off to doggy heaven, but they remain affectionately fixed in the memory of many Hamilton residents. One such animal was the Ayers' Walter, later honored by his very own book, *Walter the Improbable Hound*, written by his master Fred Ayer.

A few months after we moved to Hamilton, my personal acquaintance with Walter began. I was weeding my flower garden and he sauntered nonchalantly into the yard, looked soulfully at me with his bloodshot eyes and threw himself with a contented sigh onto the freshly planted petunia bed. A decidedly doggy smell filled the air. Nothing would rouse him; he was too fat and heavy to pick up and his skin was so loose it kept slipping from my grasp.

Walter at his ease.

Shortly afterward, my little daughter came in to report that a dog, "with all his underneaths dragging," was now on the porch. He stayed there, nestled on a bed of doll clothes, all evening and he was still there in the morning.

Later that morning, Veronica Sargent came over for a neighborly cup of coffee and I told her about the fat dog with the dragging underparts. She took a quick look and said, "Oh, that's the Ayers' dog Walter. Just call their chauffer or a taxi and they'll come and take him home."

Apparently Walter, this "noble basset hound," was known all over town, and when he overstayed his welcome, residents knew what to do. He was beloved by his owners and most of the people in town. His routine was to snarl the traffic in Depot Square in the morning and then, after a visit to his favorite restaurant for handouts or a malodorous rummage in the garbage pail, he took a long nap until supper.

# Town Talk

The following stories are by people long associated with modern town history.

## Kathryn Lamson Nickerson
*Teacher, Historian, Volunteer for All Good Causes*

Nickerson was especially fond of educating young children on the subject of town history. Her axiom was: "Today's pictures and events are tomorrow's history."

## Lawrence Lamson
*Former Selectman and Fire Chief*

The railroad has always played an important role in the town of Hamilton because it cuts right through the center of the town. The trains hold up traffic and are part of daily life. Mr. Lamson says that even now he can hardly believe that this story happened, but it did.

The Portland Express train coming from Boston around 8:30 a.m., circa 1907. *B.H. Conant Wenham Historical Association and Museum.*

*Well, it happened shortly after World War II. I was plowing for the town then. It was March and there had been quite a bit of snow as happens at that time of year, and we had just had another small storm of some six or eight inches but not too bad. That morning the train from Essex had started along on the track but got stuck in the snow a short way up.*

*I got a call that a town truck had broken down and needed a tow so I jacked up my plow and went to get him. I'm pulling him in and by then it had started to snow like a blizzard. At that time the Portland Express went through town every morning around 8:07. Well I'm coming down Walnut Street at a good clip and I see the Express up ahead pushing the Essex train along to get it off the track, and he couldn't see much in the snow, and I couldn't stop so we are coming to the crossing at about the same time and I had just gone through when the chain for the truck I was towing broke so I was on one side of the train track and he was on the other and the train rushed through.*

Larry wiped his brow in disbelief one more time as he told this story.

# Robert "Bob" Poole
*Former Police Chief*

Police work is stressful for the courageous men involved. Perhaps even more so in a small town because of the close interaction that takes place between the people and the police. Humor helps, and pranks sometimes occur.

*Eddie Hall owned a Barber Shop downtown and he was also the chief of police in Wenham, a part time position then. He was a staunch Republican and made no bones about it. Nothing about the Democrats was right or ever would be.*

*In the late 1950s Jack Kennedy was running for senator and he came through Hamilton to shake a few hands and leave some posters and bumper stickers and other Democratic promotional materials.*

*Well somehow someone put a Kennedy poster high above the mirror in Eddy Hall's shop and it stayed there for a few hours unnoticed until a Wenham selectman, also a staunch Republican, sat back in the chair for a shave. When he noticed the Democratic proclamation he left in a huff, half shaven.*

*Eddy owned horses and used to like to go to the Myopia Hunt. He had an Austin Healy with the big fenders. Somehow a big "Vote for Kennedy" sticker got under there. While Eddy was watching the Hunt, an estate owner came over to him with a quizzical look on his face.*

*"Eddy," he asked in a perplexed tone, "Are you really supporting this Kennedy?"*

*Worse was yet to come for Chief Hall. He stabled his horses on Ortins Road. One morning he arrived to care for them, only to find "Kennedy for President" banners draped over every part of the stalls. Everywhere it was possible to affix a Democratic slogan, there they were, and even the horses' rumps were not spared.*

# The Old (Retired) Librarian

For some reason many people think that the work of librarians is easy and that many spend the day reading. While most librarians do love to read, there is never time for it on the job. Work with the public is always challenging, and a librarian's work is no less so. Over the years, just about every type of unique town personality will visit the library and all of them are wonderful people. But sometimes difficult and/or comical things occur.

*One day, a very irate woman walked into the old library and threw the book she had in her hand onto the desk, where it landed with a decided thump.*

*"This book is disgusting," she said. "It has swear words in it and the Lord's name is taken in vain. I want it removed from the shelves! What is the world coming to, using our hard-earned taxes for such trash?"*

*The librarian calmly assured her that there was no need to read such material as the library was full of other more edifying books. She could leave the offending volume and they would take care of it. (She left later with another book by the same author.)*

*One day, a librarian was working in the stacks, doing inventory and weeding when a lovely middle-aged woman came up to her, leaned close and whispered in her ear, "What have you got that's spicy for a poor old widow."*

*Then there was the old gentleman from one of the estates that loved books of mystery. "Find me a good one," he'd say time after time, "and none of those written by \*&%$#\* women."*

*While story hour was going on we often had young mothers waiting for their toddlers with a newborn in their arms. Sometimes the infant thought it was time for lunch and the nursing mother would oblige. Sometimes, too, the young mom would forget where she was.*

*One day an elderly gentleman came in to use the copy machine. He placed his document down and happened to look up in time to see a full Venus de Milo figure revealed. It was unexpected, and his finger jammed onto the noisy copy machine button and page after page ground out as he stood transfixed. Without even looking up from her work, the assistant director, used to the grinding noise the old machine made, called out, "Just one push, just one push, just ONE push."*

*And then there was the elderly couple who asked that they not be called (when a reserve book came in for them) between five and six-thirty because that was when they took naps so they could stay up late to watch their favorite shows.*

# Robert "Bob" McRae
*Former Fire Chief*

Firefighting takes a toll on the lives of the valiant men involved, but sometimes humorous things happen too.

*We were at a very bad fire and the men had worked hard to keep things under control, but the flames were just too fierce. One of our men had to be evacuated and given assistance for smoke inhalation. He finally came to, and everything seemed to be all right, when he shook his head and said sincerely, "Whew, I could sure use a smoke. Has anyone got a cigarette?"*

# Edna Barney
*Teacher, Librarian and Cocurator of the Hamilton Historical Society*

This story is regarding Dr. Corcoran, who was a beloved doctor to all in town in the 1900s. He was the father of Barbara Corcoran, the former actress and writer.

> *I was just a little girl and we were having an especially bad winter with so much snow the roads could not be cleared and folks just stayed in and tried to keep warm. My sister Gertrude was weak and very sick and Dr. Corcoran had come by earlier in the week, but she was no better. After a blizzard that blocked roads everywhere, Dr. Corcoran came to our house twice on snowshoes with new medicines to care for my sister. She did get better.*

# Bibliography

Annual Reports of Town of Hamilton, 1838–2000. Hamilton Historical Society, Hamilton, MA.

Antiquarian Papers (Ipswich), Vol. IV, No. I, July 1884.

Ayer, Fred, Jr. *Walter the Improbable Hound.* Chicago: Henry Regnery Co., 1958.

Bradford, Judge Standish. Document of Massachusetts Historical Commission, May 2, 1969.

*Bylaws, Rules and Regulations to be Observed in the Town of Hamilton.* Passed April 3, 1838. Hamilton Historical Society, Hamilton, MA.

*Celebration of the Hundredth Anniversary of the Incorporation of the Town of Hamilton,* Salem, MA: Barry and Lufkin, 1895.

Dodge, H. Augusta. *Gail Hamilton: Life in Letters.* Boston: Essex Institute, 1901.

Dow, George Francis. *History of Topsfield.* Topsfield, MA: Topsfield Historical Society, 1940.

Felt, Joseph B. *History of Ipswich, Essex and Hamilton.* Cambridge, MA: Charles Folsom, 1834.

Goff, John. *Feeling for Joseph B. Felt: A Look at Salem's Early Historian and Antiquarian Preservation Perspective.* Salem, MA: n.p., 2007

Greene, Lorenzo Johnston. *The Negro in Colonial New England.* New York: Atheneum, 1968.

*Hamilton's Tercentenary 1630–1930.* Salem, MA: Newcomb and Gauss, 1930.

Landwehr, Steve. "Bradley Palmer: The Mystery Man." *Salem Evening News,* July 17, 1999.

Moran, David. *Trooper.* Boston: Quinlan Press, 1986.

Pulsifer, Janice G. *Changing Town: Hamilton, Mass. 1850–1910.* Ipswich, MA: Fox Run Press, 1976.

————. *Cutlers of Hamilton*. Salem, MA: Essex Institute Historical Collection, 1971.

————. *Gail Hamilton 1833–1896*. Salem, MA: Essex Institute Historical Collection, 1968.

————. *Robert Dodge Hamilton Minute Man*. Beverly, MA: North Shore Weeklies Publications, 1975.

*Register of the Towns of Manchester, Essex, Hamilton and Wenham, Massachusetts*. Auburn, ME: Lawton Register, 1912.

Smith, Philip Chadwick Foster. *Crystal Blocks of Yankee Coldness*. Wenham, MA: Wenham Historical Association & Museum Inc., 1962.

Tracy, Cyrus M., and Henry Wheatland. *Standard History of Essex County*. Boston, C.W. Jewett & Co., 1878.

von Meyer, George L. *Life Sketches of Leading Citizens of Essex County*. Hamilton, MA: Hamilton Historical Society, 1898.

Weeks, Edward. *Myopia: A Centennial Chronicle*. Hamilton, MA: Edward Weeks, 1985.

*Wenham in Pictures and Prose*. Wenham, MA: Wenham Historical Association and Museum, 1992.

Winthrop, John. *History of New England 1630–1649*. Vols. I and II. Boston: Thomas Wait & Son, 1826.

Wolcott, Oliver. "Down on the Farm." Report of Oliver Wolcott Building and Grounds Committee, n.d. Hamilton Historical Society, Hamilton, MA.

Young, Hammond A. "Glimpses of the Hamilton Schools 1636–1976. Unpublished paper, January 2, 1976. Hamilton Historical Society, Hamilton, MA.

Visit us at
www.historypress.net